Beauty & Desire
IN EDO PERIOD JAPAN

GARY HICKEY

■ national gallery of **australia**

Edited, designed and produced by the Publications Department of the National Gallery of Australia, Canberra
Edited by Pauline Green
Designed by Kirsty Morrison
Colour separations by Pep Colour
Printed by Inprint Limited

Cataloguing-in-Publication data
Hickey, Gary.
Beauty and Desire in Edo period Japan.

Bibliography.
ISBN 0 642 13084 1.

1. Art. Japanese – Edo period. 1600–1868 – Exhibitions.
2. Colour prints. Japanese – Exhibitions. 3. Ukiyoe – Exhibitions.
I. National Gallery of Australia. II. Title.

769.952074947

Distributed by:
Thames and Hudson (Australia) Pty Ltd,
11 Central Boulevard, Portside Business Park,
Port Melbourne, Victoria, 3207, Australia

Thames and Hudson Ltd,
30–34 Bloomsbury Street, London WC1B 3QP, UK

Thames and Hudson Inc.,
500 Fifth Avenue, New York, NY 10110, USA

ISBN in USA 0-500-97470-5
Library of Congress Catalog Card Number: 97-62528

Beauty & Desire in Edo period Japan
National Gallery of Australia, Canberra
6 June – 9 August 1998
Curator: Gary Hickey, National Gallery of Australia

Supported by The Japan Foundation

(cover) **Utagawa KUNIYASU** *Woman with umbrella* c.1820s (detail)
National Gallery of Australia (See Plate 15, page 61.)

(Plate 1) **Utagawa KUNIYASU** Edo 1794–1832
The courtesan Akome from the house of Ogiya [*Ogiya nai Akome*]
from the series *One of The Hundred and Eight Heroes of the Water Margin*
[*Tsūzoku Suikoden Gōketsu Hyakuhachinin*] c.1820s
Artist's signature: Ippōsai Kuniyasu ga   Publisher: Yorozo-ya Kichibei
Censor's seal: *kiwame*
ōban, colour woodblock print, 38.4 x 26.2cm
National Gallery of Australia, Canberra

Acknowledgements

This publication accompanies the first major exhibition of *ukiyo-e* art to be held in Australia. Neither would have been possible without the support and understanding of a number of people. Institutional support has also been integral to the success of the exhibition. Within Australia my thanks go to Dick Richards (Art Gallery of South Australia), Dr Michael Brand and Anne Kirker (Queensland Art Gallery), Clare Roberts (Powerhouse Museum, Sydney), the Art Gallery of Western Australia and the Australian National University. The National Gallery of Victoria has contributed a number of prints, many of which are being shown for the first time, including the only print by Sharaku in an Australian collection. The Art Gallery of New South Wales very generously agreed to lend a large number of important works to the exhibition including paintings and screens and I am very grateful to Jackie Menzies and Chiaki Ajioka for their ongoing support. The Los Angeles County Museum of Art was particularly helpful in organising loans from their impressive kimono collection and I thank Sharon Takeda for her prompt and professional assistance.

Private lenders have also generously contributed to the exhibition. From Australia I thank David Button, Stephanie Burns and James Gleeson. The contribution from overseas lenders has substantially enhanced the exhibition and I am very grateful to Klaus Naumann and Iwao Nagasaki, not only for lending works, but also for their enthusiasm for the project.

From within the National Gallery of Australia there are a number of people who have been closely involved with this project. I particularly thank Pauline Green and Kirsty Morrison (Publications), Harijs Piekalns (Exhibition Manager), Margaret Shaw (Research Library), Bruce Howlett (Registration) and Katinka Smith (Administration), all of whom have been closely involved with aspects of the exhibition along with the Conservation, Photography and Design sections. I would especially like to thank Robyn Maxwell (Asian Art) for her advice and suggestions and Charlotte Galloway for her continuing readiness to assist. The support of the Director of the National Gallery of Australia, Dr Brian Kennedy, has been greatly appreciated.

I am grateful for the assistance of Haruki Yoshida for many of the translations from Japanese and to Professor Tadashi Kobayashi for his professional advice and deep understanding of the subject.

Finally I would like to thank my wife Haruyo and daughter Angela for their patience and support during the long hours and lost weekends.

Gary Hickey
June 1998

CONTENTS

Plate 1

4

FOREWORD

The National Gallery of Australia is pleased to publish this book which accompanies *Beauty & Desire in Edo Period Japan*, the most significant exhibition of Edo period art yet to be held in Australia. It brings together works of the period from all of Australia's major art institutions, complemented by key loans from private and public lenders from Australia and overseas. The prints, paintings, screens and costumes trace the development of a new popular art during the Edo period (1600 – 1868) known as *ukiyo-e*, images of the 'floating world'. Selected works from the exhibition reproduced in this book include the delicately coloured images of early *ukiyo-e* artists and follow the developments and changes in *ukiyo-e* style, finishing with the bright and often confronting images of the late Edo and early Meiji period.

Beauty & Desire in Edo Period Japan has been supported by The Japan Foundation as part of their continuing program of helping to promote the understanding of Japanese culture overseas. I congratulate the curator, Gary Hickey, on his thorough research and efforts in bringing all of these works together for such a fine exhibition and publication.

Brian Kennedy
Director, National Gallery of Australia

fig.1

LOW CITY, HIGH CITY[1]

The City of Edo [*Edo no Machi*][2]

Once a small fishing village, Edo had become the most populous city in the world by the early eighteenth century, with more than one million people inhabiting an area of some 65 square kilometres situated on Edo bay at the mouth of the Sumida river [*Sumidagawa*]. The development of Edo followed the building of a castle there by the powerful feudal lord [*daimyō*] Tokugawa Ieyasu (1543–1616). Ieyasu became Japan's supreme military ruler [*shōgun*] in 1603; from that time Edo was the seat of power, a samurai city, where the elite administrative and military personnel of the *shōgun* and his *daimyō* resided. Additionally, the *daimyō* of the various provinces, along with their retinues, were obliged to spend part of their time in Edo. Their residences and samurai quarters, as well as the massive Edo castle, numerous temples and shrines, required the services of merchants, artisans and hired labourers. The lively interaction between these classes constituted a vibrant city whose influence on Japanese culture was so pervasive that the period of the Tokugawa shogunate became known as the Edo period.

Whereas struggles for power and shifting allegiances had marked earlier centuries, the Edo period (1600–1868)[3] was characterised by uninterrupted peace and relative isolation from the outside world.[4] It was as a means of maintaining peace through control of the *daimyō* that the Tokugawa shogunate devised the system known as *sankin kōtai* [alternate attendance] which required the *daimyō* and their retinues to attend the shogunal court in Edo for fixed periods. When they returned to govern their provinces, the *daimyō* had to leave their wives and children in Edo as virtual hostages. The necessity to build and maintain residential estates in Edo and pay heavy levies meant that there was a continual influx of resources from the provinces to the city. *Sankin kōtai* had the desired effect of keeping a financial check on the

daimyō,[5] but in doing so it weakened the economic and, eventually, the political power of the samurai class. Progressively the lower classes, which included the merchants and financiers, became indispensable to the growth of the capital, and these people grew increasingly wealthy. In this respect the class system that was an integral part of Edo society was turned on its head as the lowest stratum of society, the *chōnin* [townspeople], gained economic power.[6] They directed their wealth into the pursuit of pleasure, and the cultivated tastes that were fashioned around these pursuits distinguished the culture of the Edo period.

Urban culture

The combination of wealthy independent-thinking *chōnin* and the ruling samurai elite fostered the development of a vibrant new urban culture based around the *shitamachi* — the commercial districts of Edo.[7] With the greater affluence of the *chōnin* during the middle and late Edo period, the *shitamachi* became the cultural focus of city life. There, in *Kabuki* theatre, *rakugo* storytelling, the *Bunraku* puppet theatre, *geisha* arts, music of the *shamisen*, *sumo* wrestling, literature, paintings and prints, *chōnin* culture was expressed. The cultured *chōnin* also developed particular tastes in clothing and a unique manner of speech. Their aesthetic standards were defined by *asobi* [play], *iki* [chic] and *tsū* [connoisseurship].

For those living in the poorer rural villages, the bright lights of Edo offered the promise of excitement and opportunities for economic improvement. While only a few became wealthy, stories of their extravagance fuelled the dreams of the *chōnin*. Among the unfortunates of Edo society, women were particularly disadvantaged. For many, the only prospect of financial security was in the licensed bordellos of the Yoshiwara pleasure quarters.[8] It was there that the cult of the courtesan evolved, where lavishly attired women paraded and became the icons of *chōnin* culture.

Ukiyo-e and the aesthetics of *asobi*

For the *chōnin*, as for all the citizens of Edo, daily life was not without danger. The city was subjected to earthquakes, floods, storms, tidal waves and famine, and, with people living cheek by jowl in dwellings made chiefly of paper and wood, fire was the most immediate danger. In March 1657 Edo was consumed by the Meireki fire — the central government district and many downtown areas were lost, along with shrines, temples and part of Edo castle. The death toll numbered more than 100,000. However, the wealthy *chōnin* refused to be disheartened by the tenuous nature of life and continued to spend freely indulging in the pleasures available to them. To express the incongruity of their attitude to life, they appropriated the Buddhist term *ukiyo*, originally meaning 'this transient life in which we suffer', and gave it the reading 'floating world', avoiding any notion of suffering.[9] This attitude was defined by the early Edo period writer Asai Ryoi in *Ukiyo Monogatari* [Tales of the Floating World] *c.*1691:

> … living for the moment, turning our full attention to the pleasures of the moon, the snow, the cherry blossoms and the maple leaves, singing songs, drinking wine and diverting ourselves just in floating, caring not a whit for the pauperism staring us in the face, refusing to be disheartened, like a gourd floating along with the river current: this is what we call *ukiyo* …

The philosophy of living for the moment added a certain poignancy to life: it intensified delight in the transient cherry blossom, in the summer call of the cricket, and in the beauty of a young woman. Such an attitude was conducive to a life in which pleasures could be enjoyed in a sophisticated and playful manner, unfettered by daily concerns. *Asobi* [play][10] expressed itself in, and became a synonym for painting, writing poetry, music, socialising and sexual activity. Within this society the urbane sophisticate held dominion, an exemplar of the ideals of an *ukiyo* man — *iki* and *tsū*.

Entertainment in the company of youthful beauty was an essential part of Edo period pleasures. A mid-seventeenth-century screen, *Merrymaking in the garden*, depicts a scene in the Shimabara pleasure district of Kyoto where wealthy merchants and samurai are at play accompanied by charming androgynous youths. (fig.2) In the upper storey of the house a group of men concentrate on their card game, watched by a young boy with his back toward the viewer, revealing his long hair tied in a 'pony tail'. To the side, an elderly male entertainer plays the *shamisen*. In the main room downstairs the relaxed pursuits of smoking, reading poetry and drinking *sake* are enjoyed while revellers take part in a game of tug-of-war. An elderly monk is distracted from his board game of *go* by two young men who are tickling him. As a contrasting element, a solitary female beauty [*bijin*] sits aloof behind a group of men who are drinking; her hair hangs loose in the traditional classical manner. In the garden a group of samurai, identified by their swords, form a wonderful vignette as they dance to the beat of wooden clappers. Judging by the attitudes of fatigue of the palanquin bearers waiting outside the gate, the party has been a long affair. In details that would become characteristic of the *ukiyo-e* school, the artist has paid particular attention to fashion, showing the latest designs in costume and hairstyles.

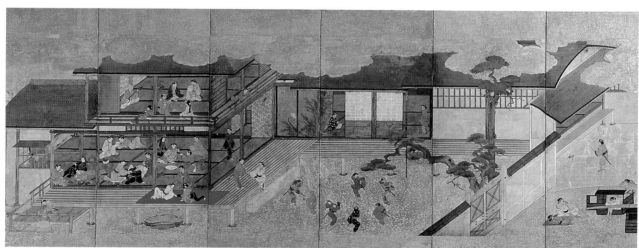

fig.2

During the Kambun era (1661–1673), young teenage dancing girls [*odoriko*] who performed at private functions reflected the taste for adolescent beauty. The popularity of charming innocence was so great that the era lent its name to this particular style of beauty, *Kambun bijin*. Characteristic of genre paintings of this era is the image of a solitary *odoriko* dancing, fan in hand, with the focus being on her stylish costume and coiffure. (see fig.1) Typically there is no indication as to the setting, although in this particular example the *koto* [Japanese harp] beside her and the mood of the poem inscribed in the upper half of the painting indicate that she is the central attraction at a social gathering, probably of a *daimyō* or a high-ranking samurai with whom this type of performance was popular. The poem translates:

Allured by the sound of a *koto*
The wind seems to come down here
Through the pine forest on the hill.
I wonder from which string the melody colours the air?

Nishiki-e

A revival of the ancient art of making woodblock prints [*hanga*] in the mid-seventeenth century gave rise to high levels of expertise and a great variety of technical developments. Monochrome woodblock prints had been used to reproduce images of Buddhist sculptures as early as the eighth century. During the Edo period the linear qualities of this simple process were envigorated, but popular demand required more colourful designs. The production of full colour prints followed the development of a technique of aligning on separate wood blocks the several sheets that correspond to the various colours of an image. The significant achievement of designing the earliest full colour prints is often attributed to Suzuki Harunobu *(1724–1770).* These prints, called *nishiki-e* [brocade pictures] because of their resemblance to a particular type of Chinese brocade, gave full expression to the costumes, make-up and coiffure of the popular figures of pleasure and entertainment. (Harunobu, *Girl teasing a cat,* fig.3)

The skilled printmaker could mimic texture by exerting pressure on the burnishing tool [*baren*], or he could add tactile beauty by blind embossing. The application of metal dust to the surface of a print added richness, as did overprinting and burnishing of black which reflected the lustrous glow

fig.3

9

fig.4

10

of lacquer ware. Overprinting was especially favoured by the later *ukiyo-e* master, Utamaro, to reveal a view as seen through a screening element such as netting (see Plate 13) or a translucent tortoiseshell comb. To express the unblemished surface of skin, areas of the finely textured hand-made paper [*washi*] were often left unprinted. When it came to expressing the delicate features of a beautiful face and an elaborate coiffure, the skills of a virtuoso wood engraver were required.

The production of *nishiki-e* was a collaborative effort between the artist, engraver and printmaker, with the design motif initiated by the publisher. While the genius of particular artists was recognised, the publisher's output was driven by public demand, thus innovation, astutely directed, was paramount.[11]

While *ukiyo-e* artists also painted pictures [*nikuhitsu*], it was in the print medium that they were best able to satisfy the tastes of the *chōnin*. For the equivalent price of a bowl of noodles or a haircut, or half the price of the cheapest admission to a *Kabuki* theatre,[12] curious townspeople could buy a print, paste it to the wall, or pass it about in order to admire and discuss the latest depictions of popular actors, or lust after beautiful courtesans while delighting in their luxurious attire. They could also purchase albums of erotic prints to be kept for private viewing at intimate moments. The ephemeral nature of this popular, affordable art symbolised the transient world of *ukiyo-e* pleasures.

Just as the archaic Buddhist term *ukiyo* had been appropriated to symbolise its antithesis, a complex labyrinth of metaphors evolved in Edo society, where the stable world became the floating world. In this fluid world of *ukiyo*, the lower class rich might be treated as nobles; and, in the pleasure quarters, courtesans cloaked in luxurious robes became goddesses of desire. (Matsuno Chikanobu, active *c.*1716–35, *Standing beauty* [*Tachi bijin*] *c.*1720s, fig.4) Obsessed with female beauty, men sought its expression in the arts; and on the stage, in the ultimate metaphor, men took the roles of women.

Notes

1. Inspired by E. Seindensticker, *Low City, High City*, Tokyo: Charles E. Tuttle, 1983.
2. Named Tokyo in 1868.
3. The Edo period is dated from 1600 when Tokugawa Ieyasu defeated his rivals at the Battle of Sekigahara. The period is alternatively dated from 1603 when Ieyasu became *shōgun* and established Edo as the seat of the Tokugawa shogunate.
4. In an attempt to strengthen its domestic authority, a policy of *sakoku*, literally 'closed country', was adopted by the Tokugawa shogunate. *Sakoku* excluded certain nationalities from Japan as well as prohibiting foreign travel by the Japanese. Domestic travel within Japan was also restricted. Until 1854 the only Western trade allowed was with the Dutch.
5. Journeys to and from the capital as well as the upkeep of two residences consumed up to 80 per cent of the *daimyō*'s income.
6. During the Edo period the Japanese class system, known as *shi-nō-kō-shō*, divided people into four classes according to their occupations — warrior, farmer, artisan, or merchant class. However, for administrative purposes the clearest distinction was between samurai and non-samurai. In the urban areas where administrative districts were known as *chō*, artisans and merchants collectively became known as *chōnin* (*nin* being the suffix for 'person') and their role was to serve the needs of the military. As cities grew the *chōnin*'s role became more autonomous.
7. Often equated with the 'downtown' of modern cities, the *shitamachi* ['low city'] was the low lying area of Edo where the commercial and manufacturing classes were required to live. The *shitamachi* was both geographically and culturally separate from the *yamanote* [foothills], the 'high city' district where the samurai class dwelt.
8. See below pp.25–35.
9. Kenneth G. Henshall points out: 'fleeting is an associated meaning with floating (note that fleet and float are etymologically the same word), with gay felt to be a further association with fleeting (from fleeting pleasures)'. Henshall, *A Guide to Remembering Chinese Characters*, Rutland and Tokyo: Charles E. Tuttle, 1990, p.560.
10. The Chinese character for 'play' is a combination of the characters for 'fluttering flag' and 'movement', meaning 'movement in a wave-like and hence indirect fashion'. Thus 'relax' or, more exactly, 'not work' is the earlier meaning of *asobi* which later became synonymous with 'play'. Ibid., p.21.
11. The artist's contribution to the production of *ukiyo-e* prints was generally acknowledged on the print, but it was not until the nineteenth century that the wood engraver's seal started to appear. The publisher's trade mark was usually located at the bottom of the print. The printmaker was rarely acknowledged. The Tokugawa authorities were sensitive to anything that would undermine their authority. For this reason, before going to publication, prints required approval. Between 1790–1874 many prints have a government censor's seal attached. From 1876 this system of censorship was abolished. See James Self and Nobuko Hirose, *Japanese Art Signatures*, Rutland and Tokyo: Charles E. Tuttle, 1987.
12. See Ellis Tinios, 'Three Early *uchiwa* Prints by Kunisada', *Andon*, 47, 1994, pp.88–93.

fig.5

MEN AS WOMEN

In Kyoto, in the early seventeenth century, on *Shijō-Gawara* [the Fourth Street Dry Riverbed[13] (of the *Kamogawa* river)] and at the Kitano Tenjin shrine, a female theatrical troupe performed, led by Okuni, a shrine attendant.[14] The roots of *Kabuki* are traced back to Okuni's popular performances, which became known as *Okuni Kabuki*.[15] The erotic nature of *Okuni Kabuki*, and its association with prostitution and vice, finally led to the banning of female performers in 1629. Subsequently, *Kabuki* theatre was performed by male youths [*wakashu*] — and so began female impersonation on the *Kabuki* stage. However, with *Wakashu Kabuki*, it was its association with pederasty that eventually led to a stipulation in 1652 requiring that all actors be adult males [*yarō*].[16] As a further measure, to make actors appear less desirable, they were required to shave off their forelocks. Following this procedure, a purple cloth was used to cover the bald patch, and it became a convention to wear the cloth even after the use of wigs was adopted.[17] Actors assuming the specialised female roles in *Yarō Kabuki* were known as *onnagata* [female-figures].

While the *odoriko* dance was performed with a certain pubescent reserve in private company, (see fig.1) the *onnagata* dance on the *Kabuki* stage reflected the *chōnin* audience's taste for the spectacular and colourful, in the dramatic expression of female poses and passions. A perfect vehicle for such a display was the *Shiokumi* [salt maidens] dance in the *Kabuki* play *Musume Dōjōji* [Daughters of Dōjō temple], with its theme of love betrayed. Based on the medieval *Nō* play, *Matsukaze*, it is the story of the Heian period (794–1185) courtier and poet Ariwara no Yukihira who was banished to Suma in western Honshū. In exile, Ariwara became infatuated with two sisters who collected buckets of brine for salt making, Matsukaze [Pine Breeze] and Murasame [Passing Shower]. When Ariwara was permitted to go back to the capital, he promised to return to Suma and, as a sign of his compact, he left his coat and cap hanging on the limb of one of the pine trees for which the area is famous. Ariwara did not return, and the two maidens were left to pine for their lost love.

Images of actors in popular roles [*yakusha-e*] was one of the major subjects of *ukiyo-e*. During the eighteenth century it was the Torii school of artists[18] who held a monopoly on this type of image. In a work by the third head of the Torii line, Torii Kiyomitsu (*c*.1735–1785), the *onnagata* Nakamura Matsue I is shown as Murasame holding the absent Ariwara's cap. (fig.6) The text indicates that the performance is the *kaomise* or 'showing of faces' at the Morita theatre — the first performance after the signing of new contracts for the year.

fig.6

To ensure the success of the new program, the cast was especially careful to impress the patrons, who in many cases were more interested in the actors than the play. Thus we are told in the inscription that their 'smiling faces are posing like daffodils in bloom'.

Nakamura Matsue wears a spectacular *furisode* [robe with 'swinging sleeves'] which symbolises youth — the crest on his sleeve identifies this famous *onnagata*. The irises decorating the sleeves are a potent symbol of masculinity; while cherry blossoms on the body of the robe symbolise femininity. His elaborate 'double dip pigtail', with its crown of combs and pins, was a popular hairstyle during the mid-eighteenth century. On stage, accompanying the *onnagata*'s expressive movements, the lyrical sounds of the *shamisen* would have evoked the weeping of the love-sick maidens.[19]

Actors strove to express the depth of the feminine psyche on many levels, even the 'supernatural' power of women, as revealed through Japanese folklore. According to legend, foxes — who had the ability to possess humans or to delude them by assuming human form — would often appear as women, for a woman's character was said to resemble the cunning fox.[20] Katsukawa Shunkō (*c.*1743–1812) has depicted the *onnagata* Nakamura Noshio in such a role. (fig.7) The actor has one hand raised and curled over like a forepaw; the chrysanthemums he holds in his other hand are possibly a reference to the fox–girl story of a prince who became infatuated with a beautiful young girl who later revealed her true identity whilst asleep in a bed of chrysanthemums.[21]

For male actors taking on female roles, styles and techniques of performance were formulated in order to mask their masculinity — types of posture, coiffure, fashion and speech were adopted to create a credible female presence on stage. Early female impersonation by *wakashu* relied on the youthful beauty of the male actors, and acting styles merely affected effeminacy. However, by the Genroku era (1688–1704), a mature style using sophisticated acting techniques to express feminine attitudes and emotions had evolved. These techniques were codified by the *onnagata* Yoshizawa Ayame I (1673–1729) in the book *Ayamegusa* [The Words of Ayame]. When discussing the *onnagata* role, Ayame maintained that

fig.7

the actor's commitment to female impersonation should extend into real life:

> … if he tries deliberately to make his integration elegant, it will not be pleasing. For this reason, if he does not live his normal life as if he were a woman, it will not be possible to be called a skillful *onnagata*.[22]

Ayame's crest of a paulownia leaf within a circle can be seen on the hairpin worn by the subject in the painting *Portrait of an onnagata* by the *ukiyo-e* artist Miyagawa Chōshun (1683–1753). (see fig.5) Here the *onnagata* demonstrates the highly stylised attitude that distinguished female impersonation. The elongated S-shaped pose is characteristic of portraits of courtesans of high rank [*tayū*]. Eyes cast down and head bowed mimic feminine bashfulness and disguise the actor's masculine chin behind the collar of his *kosode* — the precursor of the modern day kimono. In bowing his head he reveals his neck, a part of the body considered erotic — yet the fall of his hair conveniently disguises the thickness of the male neck. His shoulders are drawn back, with the chest thrust forward to suggest the swell of breasts. Knees kept close together and feet turned inwards, their masculine shape hidden beneath white *tabi* socks, complete the tail of the S-shape.[23] Arms close to the body disguise the bulk of the male torso; and one masculine hand is hidden, the other only partially revealed. The skirts of the *kosode* open sufficiently to reveal a tantalising glimpse of the underrobe. As was the convention, the actor's shaved head is concealed.[24]

In spite of these elaborate techniques, the intention was never to fully disguise the fact that the actor was a man, but to create an impression of femininity through the *onnagata*'s understanding of a woman's emotions, and his stylised expression of these emotions. The sexual ambiguity of the *onnagata*'s characterisations was keenly appreciated by the *chōnin*. In Chōshun's portrait, the actor's masculinity is acknowledged by the bold phallic-shaped *tomoe* [comma] pattern on his *kosode.*

In a genre characteristic of the later Edo and Meiji periods, Katsukawa Shunkō has depicted the *onnagata* Segawa Kikunojō as a heroic female figure.[25] In the role of the steadfast, martial woman Hangaku Gozen, in the play *Wada-gassen* [The Wada Conflict],[26] Kikunojō is able to reveal the more masculine traits of aggression and defiance. (fig. 8)

The plot concerns the events surrounding the murder of Princess Itsuki, during the reign of the third Kamakura *shōgun* Minamoto no Sanetomo (r.1203–1219). An emissary, Egara no Heita, was sent to bid for the hand of the princess, but he fell for her himself. Her rejection of his advances caused Heita to murder the princess. A servant, Asari no Yoichi, attempting to assist the *shōgun*, was barred from entering the castle because his wife, Hangaku Gozen, was a cousin of the murderer, Heita. Yoichi instantly divorced Hangaku, but she remained steadfast in her loyalty to him. In the climactic scene of the play she demonstrates this loyalty by endeavouring to break down the gates of the castle.

Kikunojō as Hangaku is shown standing tall, stripped for battle. The outer part of the *kosode* has been partially discarded,

with the sleeves tucked up and bound with a sash. With forearms protected by guards and right fist clenched, the *onnagata* is shown holding a long-handled sword [*naginata*]. To further emphasise the strength of the martial woman, Kikunojō is depicted standing barefoot in the snow.

The *Kabuki* actor's age, character and physique determined the roles in which he specialised. The *onnagata* role was the most stylised in the interpretation of a broad repertoire of types: a maiden [*musume*]; a young woman [*waka oyama*]; a matron [*kashagata*]; an old woman [*babayaku*]; and a lady of high samurai rank [*katahazushi*].[27] However, the role that provided the *onnagata* with the greatest opportunity to express the range of feminine emotion was that of the courtesan of highest rank [*tayū*] — popularly referred to as *keisei* [castle toppler].[28] In his book, Yoshizawa Ayame stressed the importance of *keisei* roles:

fig.8

… if an *onnagata* made a success of a *keisei* role, all others were easy to perform. The reason for this is that, since he is basically a man, he possesses, by his nature, a faculty of strong action, and he must carefully bear in mind the softness of the *keisei* and her feminine charm. Thus, the greatest attention should be paid to the training for *keisei* roles.[29]

There was a close association between the *Kabuki* theatre and the activities of the courtesans[30] — entertainments that the Tokugawa authorities with their pragmatic Neo-Confucian morality branded as necessary evils. Both were kept under tight government control and their activities restricted to licensed areas. Actors frequented the Yoshiwara pleasure quarters, and the love affairs between famous actors and beautiful courtesans often became *causes célèbres*. An empathy existed between the two, as *onnagata*, at least in their formative history, also worked as prostitutes and used the stage to flaunt their physical attributes. The empathy also existed on a deeper level, for *onnagata*, in a sense, entered the psyche of the courtesans, particularly when acting in dramas dealing with tragic love affairs that mirrored their real life liaisons.

Representations on stage of the lives of the courtesans also included romanticised tales of their miserable circumstances cloaked as noble sacrifice — courtesans who had not willingly chosen that profession perhaps did so through a desire to help a husband or father in need. Many of these women strove to maintain high moral standards, further enhancing the status and mystique of *tayū*.[31]

In the *Kabuki* play, *Katakiuchi Noriai-Banashi* [A Medley of Tales of Revenge], two sisters, Shinobu and Kewaizaka no Shōshō, become courtesans in the Yoshiwara in order to entrap their father's assassin, Shiga Daishichi. When Daishichi visited the bordello with a friend, the two girls took their revenge.

Tōshūsai Sharaku (active 1794–95) has shown the *onnagata* Matsumoto Yonesaburō in the role of Kewaizaka in a production of this play staged at the Kiri-za theatre. (fig.9) The actor, dressed in the elaborate style of a *tayū*, has been disturbed whilst smoking. He turns his head to look

at something occurring beyond the picture frame — perhaps the moment in the play when Daishichi enters the bordello. To add weight to the drama during such moments, actors would 'freeze' — these poses, known as *mie*, were sensational high points in the play. In this *mie*, the artist has not tried to disguise the fact that his subject is a man. He was more interested in showing the individual character of the actor than in creating an idealised portrait of beauty.[32] This psychological investigation makes Sharaku's portraiture so distinctive and interesting to modern viewers, but these representations were not popular with his contemporary audience and his output as an artist was short-lived — confined to a ten-month period.

Toward the end of the eighteenth century, the gradual debasement of the standards of the Yoshiwara courtesan[33] marked her decline as the focus of popular interest.

fig.9

Reflecting this change in taste, the *onnagata* portrayals of beautiful courtesans gave way to more dramatic roles, such as those featuring figures from the underworld. A similar trend can be seen in *ukiyo-e*, where thieves, murderers, charlatans, and evil, corrupt women were depicted with savage sensuality. The upheaval wrought by the reforms of the Meiji period (1868–1912)[34] and the accompanying loss of traditional values found *Kabuki* theatre at pains to represent the values of a changing time.[35] However, images of the *onnagata* in their stylised representation of women remain fixed in time as an important legacy of *Kabuki* tradition.

Notes continued: pages 13–17

[13] Among the lowest stratum of society were the *kawaramono* [dry riverbed people], so called after the dry riverbeds [*kawara*] where they were forced to live — they were ostracised because of the 'unclean' tasks they carried out, related to the handling of corpses and carcasses. A certain freedom accompanied this separation from the rest of society, and in their ghettos entertainment areas thrived where singers, dancers, musicians, acrobats and puppeteers performed and prostitutes plied their trade, free from government restrictions.

[14] Civil wars and natural disasters meant that as early as the Muromachi period (1378–1573) women were displaced from their homes and forced to wander the streets. This was also true of nuns and shrine attendants such as Okuni who became known as *bikuni* [itinerant nuns] and *aruki miko* [wandering shrine maidens]. They worked as prostitutes in Kyoto which became a centre of this trade. See Cecilia Segawa Seigle, *Yoshiwara: The glittering world of the Japanese courtesan*, Honolulu: University of Hawaii Press, 1993, pp.7–8.

[15] Along with *Nō* and *Bunraku* (puppet theatre), *Kabuki* is one of the three major theatrical forms of Japan. The original meaning of *Kabuki* was 'tilted', implying something strange and exotic. It was later written with different characters — *ka* meaning 'song', *bu* 'dance' and *ki* 'art'.

[16] As an adult he had the freedom to have sexual relations with *wakashu*, a choice he did not have when he was a *wakashu* himself. Paul Gordon Schalow (trans.), *The Great Mirror of Male Love*, Stanford: Stanford University Press, 1990, pp.28–29.

[17] *Ayamegusa* [The Words of Ayame], Charles J. Dunn and Bunzō Torigoe (trans.), *The Actor's Analects*, New York: Columbia University Press, 1969, pp.50–51.

[18] Torii Kiyonobu (*c*.1664–1729) who arrived in Edo from Osaka in 1689 is credited with being the founder of this family of artists.

[19] *Kabuki* music is played on stage and, as well as the *shamisen*, drums and flutes are used, accompanied by singers. A variety of other instruments provide atmospheric music and sound effects.

[20] Brenda Jordan, 'The Trickster in Japan: *Tanuki* and *Kitsune*', in Stephen Addiss (ed.), *Japanese Ghosts and Demons: Art of the supernatural*, New York: George Braziller, Inc., 1985, p.135.

[21] Henri L. Joly, *Legend in Japanese Art*, Rutland and Tokyo: Charles E. Tuttle, 7th printing 1983, p.148.

[22] Dunn and Torigoe (trans.), *The Actor's Analects* (1969), p.53.

[23] This 'pigeon-toed' stance has become characteristic of contemporary Japanese women, especially when wearing traditional footwear. *Sadoshima Nikki* (Sadshima's Diary), Charles J. Dunn and Bunzō Torigoe (trans.), 'The Secret Tradition of the *Kabuki* Dance', in *The Actor's Analects* (1969), p.159.

[24] Mark Oshima points out that the physical techniques used by the actor to show the female form required muscular tension and that this energy was an integral part of the stage presence. In discussing the training required to keep knees together (holding a piece of paper between the knees whilst moving about) he says that this was also a way of maintaining small feminine steps and keeping the hips low. Oshima, 'The Keisei as a Meeting Point of Different Worlds: Courtesan and the *Kabuki Onnagata*', in Elizabeth de Sabato Swinton (ed.), *The Women of the Pleasure Quarter: Japanese paintings and prints of the floating world*, New York: Hudson Hills Press in association with the Worcester Art Museum, Massachusetts, 1996, pp.89–93.

[25] The crest shown in this work could also identify the subject as Segawa Kikunojō III (1751–1810), who also specialised in *onnagata* roles.

[26] The plot concerns the power struggle between the Hōjō and Wada families during the early Kamakura period.

[27] These are discussed in Dunn and Torigoe (trans.), *The Actor's Analects* (1969), pp.167–168. Also known as *oyama*, *onnagata* roles were overseen by a senior *onnagata* known as a *tate-oyama*. The major subdivision of *onnagata* roles was between *waka-onnagata* [young *onnagata*] and *kashagata* [old or middle-aged female roles]. Of the former, the most prominent role was that of the extravagantly beautiful *keisei* courtesan.

[28] Seigle, *Yoshiwara: The glittering world of the Japanese courtesan* (1993), p.36 and p.17. *Keisei*, a word of Chinese origin, was originally used to describe a beautiful woman whose charm was such that she could infatuate rulers and thus bring down their kingdoms. In Japan, by the twelfth century, this term was used to describe a courtesan. *Tayū*, originally a court ranking, was adopted to designate a top-billed performer in *Nō* theatre; it was later used to refer to top-ranking courtesans.

[29] Dunn and Torigoe (trans.), *The Actor's Analects* (1969), pp.49–50.

[30] Both *onnagata* and courtesans used the high rank of *tayū*. Elizabeth de Sabato Swinton, 'Reflections on the Floating World', in de Sabato Swinton, *The Women of the Pleasure Quarter: Japanese paintings and prints of the floating world*, New York: Hudson Hills Press in association with the Worcester Art Museum, Massachusetts, 1996, p.32.

[31] Dunn and Torigoe (trans.), *The Actor's Analects* (1969), p.56.

[32] The publisher of this print was Tsutaya Jūzaburō, identified by his seal of ivy leaves under Mount Fuji. Jūzaburō was both the publisher of important *ukiyo-e* artists such as Utamaro and Sharaku and their close friend and mentor.

[33] See below pp.29–30, 34.

[34] See below p.37.

[35] Early in the Meiji period, *Kabuki* plays introduced soldiers in Western uniforms and *onnagata* dressed in Western-style costumes. Later innovations incorporated Western dramatic techniques and characterisations.

fig.10

EMBRACING DESIRE

The generative power of the sexual act has an honoured place in Japanese cultural tradition. In the myths known as the *Takamagahara* [High Plain of Heaven] cycle which tell of the origin of heaven and earth, sexual intercourse between male and female deities was the instrumental act that created the Japanese islands — an act inspired by a wagtail moving its tail feathers up and down.[36]

The native religion of Japan, *Shintō* [the way of the gods], provided a background in which physical relationships could be celebrated as natural and a gift of the gods. In *Shintō* belief all aspects of the natural world are manifestations of *kami* [gods], including the sun, moon, water, mountains and trees. Nature asserts itself in its fruitfulness — an aspect particularly relevant to an agrarian society — and the phallic shape, a symbol of nature's potency, is worshipped at festivals and ceremonies.[37] Sexual intercourse, the energetic assertion of life, has been characterised in dance, music and art by an unrestrained earthy humour.[38]

In the Edo period, the Neo-Confucianism which formed the philosophical base of the Tokugawa shogunate's power structure emphasised the maintenance of a social hierarchy; sexual liaisons were of interest to the shogunate only if they threatened to disrupt the rigid class structure.[39] Within this cultural framework, the pleasure-seeking *chōnin*, whose aspirations within society were limited by their lowly position, could embrace sexual activity, along with fashion, literature, theatre and the arts, as an expression of their lively urban culture. This aspect of *ukiyo-e* provided subject matter for novels, illustrated books, and woodblock prints.[40]

Shunga

Stories of affairs in the Yoshiwara pleasure quarters provided the material for popular tales known as *ukiyo-zōshi* [books of the floating world].[41] There were also guide books, some of which specialised in giving instruction as to the correct behaviour on visits to the pleasure quarters, as well as providing critiques of the courtesans. Erotic images formed an important part of these literary works, with the popularity of *ukiyo-zōshi* due in part to monochrome illustrations by such early *ukiyo-e* masters as Hishikawa Moronobu (*c.*1618–1694) (see fig.11) and Sugimura Jihei (active *c.*1691–97).

The Japanese term for erotic pictures was *makura-e* [pillow pictures]; they also became popularly known as *higa-e* [secret pictures], or by the Chinese-derived term, *shunga* [spring pictures] — the vitality of spring growth symbolising youth, puberty and arousal of sexual desire.[42] Desirable young women (and men) were alluded to as flowers, with the quintessential symbol of Japan, the briefly flowering cherry-blossom, signifying the ephemeral nature of their beauty.[43]

The erotic symbolism of such associations is given expression in a print by the early *ukiyo-e* master, Suzuki Harunobu (1724–1770), which shows a young man struggling with a girl in an attempt to retrieve a love letter. (fig.12) In the background their youthful virility is referred to in both visual and literary terms, for under a delicate plum blossom water gushes from a bamboo pipe, and in the clouds above a poem, signed Chōsui, reads:

> Stretching across scarlet plum blossoms,
> Bamboo pipes are green.[44]

fig.11

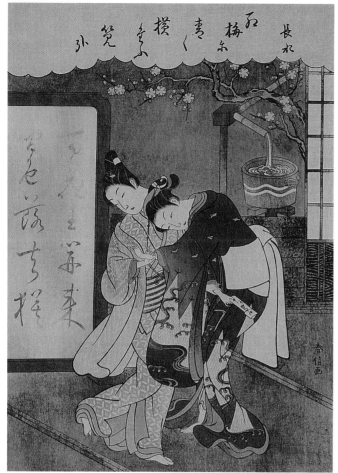

fig.12

The girl's youthfulness is further emphasised by the 'swinging sleeves' of her costume [*furisode*], decorated along the hem and on the sleeve with the traditional subject of plovers and waves, in this case against a background of fishing nets hung out to dry.[45]

Veiled sexuality was not only used as a means of titillation. In times of government control of erotica it also helped to maintain popular interest in *ukiyo-e* prints.[46] Pictures that provided erotic glimpses of female flesh were known as *abuna-e* [dangerous pictures], and were legally produced. An *abuna-e* by Harunobu shows a courtesan 'stepping' into the narrow picture frame and — in what was to become a convention with *ukiyo-e* artists — revealing a delicate white ankle. (fig.13) In the accompanying poem, her beauty is compared to one of the six rivers of different provinces celebrated for their purity. In the upper part of the picture there is a portrait of the poet Minamoto no Toshiyori (1055?–1129?), whose poem translates:

fig.13

20

Tomorrow I will come
Here to the Noji-Tama river
Walking over the hagi plants
The moon will harbour in its sparkling ripples.

In a 'city of bachelors', where men outnumbered women, opportunities for dalliance in everyday life were infrequent and the Yoshiwara pleasure quarters provided an officially sanctioned outlet for pent up male desires. A convoluted etiquette relating to entry to the exclusive inner sanctums of the Yoshiwara meant that only the very rich could indulge after following a prescribed set of procedures largely designed to relieve them of their money. The sexual act itself was the culmination of numerous introductions which had the effect of heightening desire and adding to the mystique of the courtesan.

Money alone did not allow unrestricted access to the Yoshiwara; the patron also needed to know how to behave in the manner of a sophisticate, a *tsū*, equal to the refined social graces of the top ranking courtesan. If not, he ran the risk of being branded as a *yabo*, a boorish fellow reeking of rustic uncouthness.[47] Thus, although sexual activity was the main business of the pleasure quarters, for the cultured *chōnin* the intricacies of Yoshiwara protocol became a means of refined cultural expression.

As early as the Nara period (710–794) illustrated sex manuals had existed.[48] During the Edo period, albums of *shunga* might still fulfil this function by being instructional as well as

fig.14

titillating. In a voyeuristic manner and with extraordinary imagination and extravagant detail, *shunga* albums led the viewer through a series of pictures of foreplay. Thus we see images of struggle as a prelude to the sexual act in the works of Harunobu. One such print shows a servant disturbing a masked man, perhaps a samurai or even a *daimyō* not wishing to reveal himself at play with a courtesan. (fig.14) And in the print of the young man trying to retrieve what is probably a love letter, there is an innocent sexuality in the 'passionate dance' of the boy and girl. (see fig.12) Works such as these were the mildly erotic frontispieces to *shunga* albums that went on to reveal the culmination of carnal desire.

In a print by Keisai Eisen (1790–1848) — possibly a frontispiece to a *shunga* album — a typical Eisen beauty, distinguished by her long thin face, rests her elbow on a brazier cover as she leans suggestively over her lover, whispering risqué remarks — the title of this twelve-print series is *Keisei higo* [A Beauty's Lewd Words]. (see fig.10) The couple, ensconced within the confines of a pleasure boat in mid-winter, contain their warmth beneath a quilt; the flushed face of the courtesan suggests that her inflamed passions will provide sufficient warmth for both. She holds a wad of tissue, known as 'paper for the honourable act' [*onkotogami*] — a typical erotic detail. The Chinese character *sen* on the corner of the quilt covering the courtesan reveals that the artist is Eisen. [49]

While artists would sometimes conceal a signature within the body of a work, they seldom identified themselves as the designers of *shunga*, and attribution is based on stylistic grounds alone. Although sumptuary laws were issued in the early eighteenth century, the authorities rarely prosecuted publishers for producing explicit erotic prints;[50] artists remained cautious nevertheless.

In an explicit *shunga* print by Hosoda Eishi (1756–1829), a man is engaged in foreplay. (fig.15) The couple kiss, using the tongue — a technique that was considered exotic and recommended by many handbooks as a means of stimulating a timid or passive woman. Their conversation, recorded in the script above, has the woman pleading for the man to return, and the man commenting: 'You seem to be new here, you don't seem to be a professional.'

fig.15

In the Yoshiwara, in order to maintain business, courtesans were taught the art of deceit. Here the courtesan has amply fulfilled her function as a professional by creating an illusion of both innocence and unbridled passion. More importantly, by pleading for him to come again, she has convinced her client of her love for him, which means that he probably will return, and thus business will prosper. [51]

Images of illicit affairs in the world outside the pleasure quarters were also produced to entertain and to arouse. In a print from the *shunga* series *Tsuma-gasane* [Overlapping Skirts], Katsushika Hokusai (1760–1849) depicts a married woman in a dalliance with a lusty male. (fig.16) The woman's husband is apparently away at a hot springs resort. While she uses her husband's lack of virility as an excuse for her infidelity,

the man does not believe her and claims that her sexual appetite has weakened her husband. Both are aroused by this conversation, and the episode is brought to a noisy climax — described in detail in the Japanese script which forms an important part of the composition, leaving no space unfilled. The figures themselves are barely contained within the picture frame and the frenetic lines of the discarded clothing reflect the lines of script above. In his *shunga* Hokusai used the technique of filling the entire picture frame[52] in order to confront the viewer. Genitalia are exaggerated, not through any lack of understanding of anatomy but as a visual expression of emotional intensity.

The innocent sexual curiosity of loving couples that characterised early *shunga*, by Hokusai's time had become frenzied scenes of wild fornication that focused more on the lewd or brutal side of sexuality. In the second half of the nineteenth century, with the new Meiji government attempting to adopt Western political and social values and increasingly self-conscious of Japan's image on the international stage, the institution of the Yoshiwara became a national embarrassment;[53] and *shunga* presented an image of cultural mores with which the government was uncomfortable. Although the earthy sensuality that had long characterised Japanese society remained, there was no official acknowledgement of its existence.

fig.16

36 These myths were chronicled in two literary sources, the *Kojiki* (AD 712) [Records of Ancient Matters] and the *Nihon Shoki* (AD 720), [Chronicle of Japan] also known as the *Nihongi*.

37 The *Shintō* phallic deity is known as *konsei* and is worshipped as the god of childbirth and marriage. Just as the phallus became a symbol of nature's potency, the female generative organ was also celebrated — in shrines the red painted gate-like structure, or *torii*, symbolises the female 'birth passage'. Phillip Rawson, *Oriental Erotic Art*, London: Quartet Books Ltd, 1981, p.126.

38 Buddhism, introduced into Japan in AD 552, had no moral laws against sex either.

39 In a system where the interests of the group were paramount, values such as self-sacrifice, faithfulness and loyalty had more importance than Western notions of personal sin, conscience and atonement.

40 The Japanese attitude to sex along with other bodily functions had an uninhibited robust flavour to it. Depictions of unrestrained sexual activity date back to as early as the tenth century with drawings known as *warai-e* [laughing pictures] of members of the Buddhist clergy indulging in sexual acts with aristocratic ladies. There was also a tradition, initiated by Abbot Toba (*Kakuyū* 1053–1140) of farcical handscrolls depicting contests where the participants propelled flatus against one another [*he-gassen*] or compared relative phallus sizes [*yōbutsu kurabe*].

41 What is considered to be the first work of this genre, *Kōshoku Ichidai Otoko* [Life of an Amorous Man] 1682, by Iharu Saikaku (1642–1693), is a collection of comic anecdotes set in the pleasure quarters.

42 One Japanese word for prostitute, *baishunfu*, in Chinese *mai-chun-fu*, literally translates as 'sell-spring-girl'. John Stevenson, *Yoshitoshi's Women: The woodblock print series 'Fuzoku Sanjuniso'*, Colorado: Avery Press, Inc., 1986, p.19. Stevenson also states that the earliest reference to *shunga* comes from China where the Sung dynasty (AD 960–1279) term *chun-gong-hua* referred to 'pictures of [sexual dalliances in] the Spring Palace'.

43 In this context *uba-zakura*, or 'old woman-cherry blossom' is a euphemism for a faded beauty, a 'has-been'. Taken further in sexual imagery refined phrases from the natural world, such as 'the dew in the peony', became euphemisms for the sexual organ. In a hanging scroll by Kitagawa Fujimaro (1790–1850) titled *Man strolling with a boy carrying branches* c.1810, a young man and boy are depicted in a composition similar to that of a courtesan and her attendant. The attractions of both male and female youths are described in an attached poem which contrasts the sexual allure of the courtesan (equated with the cherry blossom) and that of the young man (equated with the blossoms of the young plum). Donald Jenkins, *The Floating World Revisited*, Portland: Portland Art Museum in association with University of Hawaii Press, 1993, p.196–197, catalogue IV–4. In early *ukiyo-e* images such as those of Harunobu the distinction between the sexes is minimised. If not for differences in clothing and hairstyle the equal prominence given to both sexes' adolescent charms would make it impossible to distinguish between them (except in *shunga* where genitalia reveal the obvious).

44 Henshall, *A Guide to Remembering Chinese Characters* (1990), p.13. The green of this poem in Japanese reads as *ao* which most commonly translates as 'blue'. The modern character for *ao* derives from two earlier Chinese characters, one meaning 'growing plant life' or 'life', and the other 'growth around a full well' which is 'fresh' and 'green'. For this reason *ao* is also a metaphor for 'immature' and 'young'. In this light the symbolism of the phallic-shaped 'green' bamboo bursting with fecundity becomes more apparent.

45 See the entry 'Plovers', in *Japan: An illustrated encyclopedia*, Tokyo: Kodansha, 1993, p.1208. In Japan the plover, a shorebird, was a common subject for poetry. The 'plover and wave' pattern was also widely featured on *kosode* and in the decorative arts.

46 The Kyōhō Reforms (1716–36) banned erotica as detrimental to public morals, however erotic works continued to be produced and were tolerated by the Tokugawa authorities.

47 By the late Edo period the rigidly formal language and manner of the samurai epitomised all that defined a *yabo*. This was especially true of rural samurai. Seigle, *Yoshiwara: The glittering world of the Japanese courtesan* (1993) p.136.

48 See the entry 'Shunga', in *Japan: An illustrated encyclopedia* (1993), p.1425. During the eighth century illustrated sex manuals such as the *osokuzu no e* [posture pictures] were required by law as essential reading for physicians. Another sex manual, the *Eisei hiyō shō* [Secret Essentials of Hygiene] was presented to the throne in 1288.

49 The character is placed next to another commonly used as a suffix for ship [*maru*] (a reference to the pleasure craft carrying the two lovers) thereby disguising Eisen's signature within the title of this illicit work.

50 S.E. Thompson, 'The Politics of Japanese Prints', in Dawn Lawson (ed.), *Undercurrents in the Floating World: Censorship and Japanese prints*, New York: The Asia Society Galleries, 1991.

51 Courtesans learnt deceit by consulting *showake*, books on love-making techniques such as *Kosogurigusa* [Tickling grass] 1654, and *Hidensho* [Secret teachings] c.1640 – 'how to cry when parting with a patron'. Seigle, *Yoshiwara: The glittering world of the Japanese courtesan* (1993), p.190.

52 The technique of filling the entire picture plane with a figure was also used by Utamaro in his *ōkubi-e* [bust portraits].

53 The Japanese government was forced to acknowledge the bondage of the Yoshiwara courtesans following a diplomatic crisis in 1872 when the Peruvian government raised the issue of the Japanese trade in prostitutes. Although it had been cloaked as 'term employment', the Japanese admitted that the selling of women into the Yoshiwara had amounted to slavery, and this 'trading of human beings' was redressed in the Prostitute Emancipation Act of 1872.

fig.17

PLEASURE TOWN[54]

An Edo bordello owner and an astute entrepreneur, Shōji Jin'emon, wrote to the authorities in 1612 asking for a licence to operate his business in a restricted area of Edo. In doing so he was drawing on a common practice of establishing licensed prostitution quarters in large cities.[55] Jin'emon persuaded the government to accept his proposal, arguing that containing the licensed quarters within one area would enable the authorities to maintain surveillance of any subversive elements.[56] Permission was given in 1617 and an area of swampy land was allocated. The land was drained and filled and named Yoshiwara, or 'reed plain', after the reeds that grew there in abundance.

In 1657 the Yoshiwara was destroyed in the disastrous Meireki fire.[57] A new Yoshiwara was built, consisting of 20 acres in Asakusa, a considerable distance from Edo city.[58] Its geographical isolation became a metaphor for a closed society that developed its own code of conduct, language and culture. In plan the new pleasure quarters were modelled on the original Yoshiwara, with a broad central boulevard, the Nakanochō, and side streets laid out in a grid pattern. In order to keep an eye on customers and to stop courtesans from escaping, the new quarters were enclosed within walls and surrounded by a deep moat. The only access was through the great gate, the ōmon, which was guarded and closed at night.

Images produced in the late Edo period give an idea of the physical environment of the Yoshiwara.[59] Utagawa Hiroshige, (1797–1858) in his series *Meisho Edo hyakkei* [One Hundred Famous Views of Edo], depicted many scenes in and around the pleasure quarters. *Kakuchū shinonome* [Dawn in the licensed quarters] shows weary revellers making their way home through one of the many side streets running off the Nakanochō. (fig.17) It is spring and the cherry trees planted on either side of the gate are in bloom. Government regulation did not permit the permanent planting of cherry trees in the Yoshiwara, so trees in bud were brought in each year and put in place in time for the cherry blossom festival. Like the courtesans whose beauty they signified, after the trees had served their purpose they were discarded. At the time Hiroshige produced this series, the heyday of the Yoshiwara had passed and his depictions of the licensed quarters suggest a sense of nostalgia for past pleasures. When he began the series in 1857, Hiroshige was an old man and his introspection and solitude are reflected in the transient blossoms and the revellers departing.

Regardless of its geographical and social isolation, city men flocked to the night life of the Yoshiwara. They travelled there on foot or on horseback, by palanquin or by fast river taxi — alighting at the mouth of the San'ya canal. (Hiroshige, *Night view at Matsuchi Hill and the San'ya Canal*, fig.18.)

fig.18

25

Along the way they may have stopped for refreshments at one of the many teahouses that lined the route, or to disguise themselves or tidy up at a point known as *Emonzaka* [Sprucing hill]. At the great gate they were required to identify themselves to the keeper and leave their weapons.

Once inside the Yoshiwara, an array of pleasures awaited those who could afford to indulge. At a house of assignation [*ageya*], the very rich could meet with a top ranking courtesan [*tayū*]. Less affluent customers made their way directly to one of the bordellos where courtesans of lower ranks were displayed behind latticed screens. The even less fortunate looked on, dreaming of what could never be. In 1689 the *ukiyo-e* writers, Ihara Saikaku and Isogai Sutwaka, described the procession of a *tayū* to an assignation with a rich patron and the inflamed passions such a display aroused:

> When a courtesan has a client, she dresses in fine apparel of original design, for instance, in the very popular dark purple silk covered with minute white tie-dye points, and she parades to an *ageya*, kicking a foot outward at each step as in a figure-eight, holding her shoulders straight and twisting her hips. A crowd of spectators gathers to watch her. From the bordello to the *ageya*, it is scarcely a hundred and twenty yards, but the courtesan walks so slowly and solemnly, it can take two hours on a long autumn day; the *ageya* proprietor has a hard time appeasing a short-tempered patron.

But a procession can be the beginning of an important love affair, an opportunity to impress and entice men. The courtesan arranges her clothing so that her red crêpe de chine undergarment will flip open to reveal a flash of white ankle, sometimes as high as her calf or thigh. When men witness such a sight, they go insane and spend money they are entrusted with, even if it means literally losing their heads the next day. But most men who stand on the street to watch the procession are lightweights who cannot afford to buy these women; they only gape, envious of the men who can pay the courtesan's price.[60]

Many of the women of the Yoshiwara were themselves children of prostitutes. Life may have been hard for these women, so was life for the majority of Japanese during the Edo period.

fig. 19

Reflecting this hardship, many destitute families, especially from rural areas where natural disasters hit hardest, were forced to sell their daughters into prostitution. The girls were contracted to work in the bordello for a fixed period, usually ten years, and for this service the parents received *minoshirokin* [money for the body]. Although saddened by their loss, a daughter's sacrifice might be seen as a noble act — a theme lauded in popular fiction, on the stage, and in *ukiyo-e*.

One of the most popular of these tragic stories was of a self-sacrificing courtesan of noble breeding, Komurasaki, and her lover, Hirai Gonpachi, a handsome but misguided outcaste of society. Gonpachi, a samurai, was said to have killed a man in his home province. Escaping to Edo, he became a *rōnin* [literally 'floating man'], a masterless samurai. At an inn he befriended the young Komurasaki, who had been kidnapped by criminals. She warned Gonpachi of their evil intent towards him, and in turn he rescued her, and returned her to her parents. Later, Komurasaki's family, then stricken by poverty, was forced to sell her into the pleasure quarters where she rose to the high rank of *tayū* in the Great Miura bordello. Gonpachi, who had become a frequent visitor to the Yoshiwara, again met Komurasaki and they fell deeply in love. To buy his lover's freedom Gonpachi resorted to robbery and murder, but he was caught and beheaded for his crimes. The devastated Komurasaki had her contract purchased by a wealthy patron and, that same night, committed suicide over her sweetheart's grave.

In the print *Komurasaki and her lover Gonpachi*, Tamagawa Shūchō (active 1790–1803) has used the vertical *hashira-e* [pillar print] format as a means of linking two figures (fig.19) — a format made popular by Utamaro. Komurasaki is about to pass a pipe to her lover, yet they seem almost oblivious of one another, distracted by some action beyond the picture frame. On reading the title, the Edo public would have been well aware of the tragedy underlying this seemingly quiet moment.

Embellished stories of the lives of famous courtesans strengthened the cult of the Yoshiwara and enhanced the mystique of the *tayū*, effectively setting these women in a class apart from their unlicensed competitors outside.

fig.20

The Japanese, who had a propensity for ranking, extended this practice to the Yoshiwara, and courtesans were graded according to their attributes. In the pleasure quarters, as with society in general, ritual and dress signified rank. The elaborate formality associated with the gorgeous costume, hairstyle and make-up of the *tayū* created the impression of a unique, desirable and, consequently, fabulously highly-priced 'product'. *Ukiyo-e* prints played their part in publicising the pleasures of the Yoshiwara and advertising the best merchandise. (See Kikugawa Eizan 1787–1867, *Yoru–inu no koku* [Evening, hour of the dog], fig.20.)

As well as being renowned for their beauty and lavish dress, the *tayū* were skilled in the traditional arts of tea ceremony, flower arranging and calligraphy. Amongst other skills desirable in a courtesan of high rank were *shamisen* and flute playing, singing, dancing, playing the board game of *go*, painting,

fig.21

day of the new year. (fig.21) She is wearing eight layers of *kosode*, the outer layer is decorated with a tie-dyed design of a peacock, the traditional motif of the house of Matsubaya. Her *obi* demonstrates extravagant taste, utilising a full width of damask silk, decorated with the traditional Chinese motif of a dragon soaring amongst clouds and cavorting with a flaming disc. A crown of ornamental hairpins and two tortoiseshell combs adorn her elaborate hairdo with its imposing side pieces.

composing *haiku* poems and fortune telling. They were also expected to be able to engage in witty repartee with their clients. A high rank could be raised further by attachment to a line of famous names — given to only the most beautiful and skilled courtesans of a particular house. Published directories listed these women and their particular attributes.

After the 1750s the rank of *tayū* was replaced by that of *oiran*.[61] In a painting by Utagawa Toyoharu (1735–1814), a sumptuously attired *oiran* is seen stepping out on the first

fig.22

A fair complexion is one of the most desirable attributes of a Japanese woman[62] and this *oiran*'s unblemished white skin is enhanced by cosmetics. White powder [*oshiroi*] was used for the face, the throat, the chest, the nape of the neck, the hands and feet.[63] Bare feet were considered to be alluring, especially, as in this case, when seen against a crimson silk undergarment. Sometimes the toenails were painted. The *oiran*'s small, delicate lips are highlighted with rouge derived from the juice of safflower and applied with the third (ring) finger, the 'rouge-marking-finger'. To mask the prominence of an often fleshy lower lip, this was covered with *oshiroi* before applying rouge. Red, considered an erotic colour by the Japanese, symbolises the transition to womanhood; more vibrant in contrast with the purity of white, the combination of the two was considered especially alluring.[64]

In a print of an equally gorgeous *oiran* by Eizan, (fig.22) the crescent moon shape of her painted eyebrows imparts a youthful naivety.[65] Desirable almond-shaped eyes are also highlighted with black. Given particular attention are alluring details of her hair — the downy hair of her sideboards, the tuft at the nape of her neck, and the hair at her forehead forming the highly desirable projecting peak known as the 'wild goose'. In keeping with the practice in vogue, her lower lip is painted with an iridescent greenish rouge and her teeth are blackened.[66] On ceremonial occasions a haughty appearance was achieved with a coiffure piled high, and by wearing elevated clogs.

To be properly trained in Yoshiwara language,[67] manners and customs, promising young girls of seven or eight, whether sold by their parents through economic necessity or children of the quarters, were apprenticed to high ranking courtesans. It was customary for a courtesan to have two apprentices [*kamuro*] who would be matched in terms of age and physical appearance and given names that formed a pair. In most cases the courtesans took care of their charges and in a sense acted as surrogate elder sisters. At thirteen or fourteen the *kamuro* became fully fledged prostitutes and were referred to as *shinzō*, a nautical term originally meaning 'newly launched boat' but in this instance 'newly-made'. To mark this transition a girl's teeth were blackened, the dye being collected from

seven friends and the cost sponsored by a couple known as *kane-oya* [iron parents] after the metal from which the dye was derived.[68]

The relationship between the courtesan and her *kamuro* is the subject of a print from an untitled series by Utagawa Kunisada I (1786–1864), printed almost exclusively in shades of Prussian blue. (fig.23) Two young *kamuro* peek from behind the skirts of their mistress, Kaomachi of the Tama-ya bordello. They are shown parading along the central street of the Yoshiwara pleasure quarters, the Nakanochō, with stylised cherry blossoms against a graded black background. To give further emphasis to the close relationship of the three, Kunisada has created a design weaving the matching patterns of their *kosode*.

Bijin-ga of the period illustrate that by the mid-eighteenth century the costume and make-up of the courtesan of high rank had become so ostentatious that she was unrecognisable as a real woman. Her degeneration was lamented by contemporary writers — in 1763 Hara Budayū wrote:

fig.23

In the old days, prostitutes considered it unattractive to make up their faces with rouge and powder, and even those high-class courtesans who put on light makeup for trips to the *ageya* were scorned as 'common'. The high-ranking courtesan's hair was casually and simply combed, and tied in a Hyōgo knot, and only this characteristic hairstyle and the light rouge on their toenails and the beautiful slippers that hid their toes set courtesans apart from ordinary townswomen. But now, their fashion is to plaster their hair with grease. They display seven or eight decorated hairpins, and wear two or three huge combs that look like cleats of wooden clogs.[69]

The popular ideal of beauty was mutable, indicative of a floating world that did not wish to delve into the depths of reality. The use of cosmetics to mask and then delineate desirable features was an indicator of popular taste, as were the hairstyles that went through a variety of dramatic changes in the Edo period. Costume, which provided the greatest scope for exploiting popular taste, was an essential element in expressing the Edo aesthetic. Although the basic shape of the *kosode* did not change,[70] features such as the length of the sleeve and its width, and the length, width and tie of the *obi*, played an important part in the evolution of surface design. Using techniques such as gold leaf, embroidery, ink painting and diverse resist dye methods, *kosode* were adorned with motifs commonly seen in *ukiyo-e*. The Japanese obsession with nature dominated these motifs. Designs also featured auspicious symbols drawn from the natural and the mythological worlds, famous locales, scenes relating to classical literature, and an almost playful use of both Chinese and Japanese characters — as much for their decorative qualities as their literal meaning. Motifs from the everyday world were also used chiefly for their decorative appeal.

Present day perception of the vibrant culture of the Edo period is somewhat restricted when it comes to costume, for extant *kosode* are generally the costumes of the very rich or the privileged. However, the rise in wealth of the merchant class meant that those who were less bound by tradition set the trends in fashion. Their innovative designs filtered upwards and the taste we see expressed in surviving *kosode* reflects the merchant class taste for the highly decorative.

fig.24

At the pinnacle of popular taste, the top ranking courtesans and *onnagata* defined what was chic. The series *Hinagata wakana no hatsu moyō* [New Designs as Fresh as Young Leaves] by Isoda Koryūsai (active *c.*1764–88) shows contemporary fashion modelled by famous courtesans. These prints were specifially produced to introduce the latest designs available in fabric shops and to attract orders (designs could also be chosen from published sample books). In a print from the series, the courtesan Kisakata of the Obishi-ya bordello is dressed in a new *kosode* design; another design can be seen on the *kosode* hung over a clothes rack. (fig.24) These prints were so well received that the publisher urged Koryūsai to continue the series; it was later continued by the young Torii Kiyonaga (1752–1815), with about 110 prints produced in all.

Analysis of character by physical appearance was idiomatic of the work of Kitagawa Utamaro (1753–1806) during the Kyōwa era (1801–1804), a period in which the artist often signed his prints *Kanso Utamaro* [Utamaro the physiognomist]. In his series of portraits of ten women, *Saki-wake kotoba no hana* [Variegations of Blooms According to Their Speech], he attempts as well to extrapolate character traits by attaching the women's spoken words. He draws further parallels by enclosing flowers within the title cartouche, each bloom matched to a particular character type. In the print, *Adamono* [The coquettish woman], a narcissus flower refers to the flighty nature of this woman, also revealed by her words.[71] (fig.25)

In *ukiyo-e* very few artists sought to portray the harsh realities of courtesans' lives, simply because this was not what the market demanded.[72] Even when social conventions allowed for depictions of the lowest class of prostitute, the streetwalker,

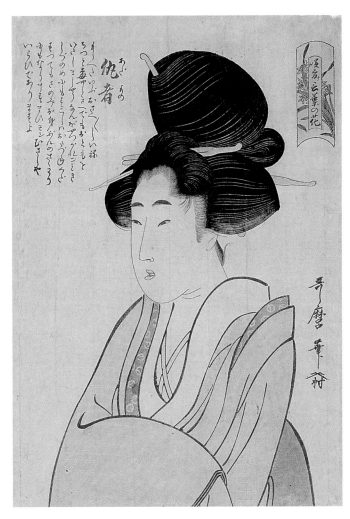

fig.25

these images, like the prostitute's made-up skin, were glossed over to disguise the miserable existence of the subject — or the syphilitic sores, the real 'flowers'[73] of her trade.[74]

In a print from his series featuring popular female *Kabuki* roles, *Mitate yami tsukushi* [*Mitate* (parody) Variety of Darkness], Utagawa Kunisada I has portrayed an *onnagata* in the role of a streetwalker furtively glancing about for customers. (fig.26) The moonlit night throws deep shadows, and silhouettes the figures of the Edo citizens out for an evening stroll. At the same time the moonlight accentuates the distinctive thick white make-up worn by the *onnagata*. With a straw mat, used as bedding, the prostitute stands apart from the crowd beneath the branches of a willow tree — a traditional symbol of prostitution adopted from China. The headscarf held between the teeth, ostensibly to stop it from being blown away, was also an erotic gesture. Strong emotions were concealed by biting something, such as a sleeve or a tissue, and women shown doing this were understood to be of a passionate nature. The Meiji period artist Tsukioka Yoshitoshi (1839–1892) has used these conventions in his romanticised portrait of a streetwalker from the series *Tsuki hyakushi* [One Hundred Phases of the Moon]. (fig.27) The accompanying poem by the female poet Oshun Hitotose translates as:

> Like reflections in the rice-paddies
> the faces of streetwalkers in darkness
> are exposed by the autumn moonlight.[75]

Courtesans completed their contract with the bordellos at the age of twenty-seven and, although an unfortunate few found themselves working on the streets, in a society with an excess of men most ended up as concubines or wives of their former patrons. Others, still indebted to their employers, found work in different capacities within the Yoshiwara. Whatever their circumstances, courtesans of high rank, with their cloistered existence, refined tastes and relatively pampered lifestyle, were at odds with society in general, and at the age of twenty-seven the prospect of future life in the real world must have seemed daunting. An unusually revealing painting by Katsukawa Shun'ei (1762–1819) depicts a courtesan who has reached the end of her tenure at the Yoshiwara. (see fig.29)

fig.26

fig.27

At different times during the Edo period, red was a prohibited colour for *kosode*,[76] thus, in a daring and incongruous gesture, Shun'ei has depicted this frail beauty exposing the vibrant red lining of her *kosode* — here worn inside out. Her painted white skin seems to glow with a sensual vulnerability, set against the red, the deep lacquer-like black of her oiled coiffure and the neutral yellow tones of the silk ground. As a counterpoint, the whiteness of her bare neck is revealed as she bends forward to look in angst at a letter spread out before her. Her contorted posture, clenched fingers and contracted eyebrows reflect the mood of the accompanying poem by Ota Nampo (1749–1823):

> Courtesans of the five streets of the quarter,
>
> ten years adrift on an ocean of troubles,
>
> released at twenty-seven with misguided dreams.
>
> Ah! This bitter mirage of the bordellos.[77]

Around the middle of the Edo period the popularity increased of a type of female entertainer known as *geisha* [skilled person]. These women, accomplished in the art of music, singing, dancing and witty repartee, were hired to entertain at parties both inside and outside the Yoshiwara.[78] They were more restrained in the style of their costumes and coiffure than their showy sisters in the licensed quarters, and although they were not meant to sleep with their customers, their beauty, skill and charm made them objects of desire. In *Cotton-goods Street, Odenma-chō* from the series *Meisho Edo hyakkei* [One Hundred Famous Views of Edo], Hiroshige has depicted two *geisha* holding the hems of their *kosode* high as they emerge from the entrance to the cotton merchants' quarter, in downtown Edo. (fig.28) It was customary to walk in twos in order to avoid compromising situations. However, the two depicted would have attracted attention because of the disarray of their coiffure and their lively interaction, indicating that they are slightly inebriated after providing the evening's entertainment.

fig.28

fig.29

and dance were permitted to remain and their refined skills increased their status and popularity, eclipsing the now debased courtesan.

In 1842, as part of the *Tempō* reforms, pictures of courtesans, *geisha* and actors were banned, marking the demise of a subject matter that had already fallen from favour. Although both the Yoshiwara and illustrations of the courtesans experienced a revival after the period of the *Tempō* reforms, neither reached their earlier peaks of refinement. The social and political upheaval that characterised nineteenth-century Japan saw a change in artistic taste and direction that would relegate images of elegant Yoshiwara beauties to the distant past.

Notes continued: pages 25–34

[54] Licensed quarters were variously known as *yūkaku* [play quarter], *kuruwa* [licensed quarter], or *iromachi* [pleasure town].

[55] The first walled-in pleasure quarter in Japan was the Shimabara in Kyoto, established in 1589. Osaka also had its own pleasure quarter, known as the Shinmachi.

[56] The greatest threat to security was from the *rōnin*, masterless samurai who had been displaced by the shift in power following the victory of Tokugawa Ieyasu. Their marginalisation bred discontent and many became involved in criminal activity and sedition. This culminated in an abortive *rōnin* uprising (the Keian incident) in 1651. Bordellos provided ideal hiding places for *rōnin*.

[57] See above p.8

[58] This became known as Shin [new] Yoshiwara, the former location being referred to as Moto [original] Yoshiwara.

[59] At this time portraits of courtesans and actors were not officially sanctioned and pictures of scenic locales became fashionable.

[60] *Shin-Yoshiwara Tsunezunegusa* [Perennial grass of the New Yoshiwara] by Ihara Saikaku and Isogai Sutwaka, 1689, Teihon Saikaku zenshū, 6:253. Quoted by Seigle, *Yoshiwara: The glittering world of the Japanese courtesan* (1993), p.77.

[61] Ibid., pp.229–232. Before the 1750s the various classes of courtesan in order of ranking were *tayū*, *kōshi*, *sancha*, *tsubone* and *hashi*. After the 1750s under the general term of *oiran* (a contracted form of *oira no*, meaning 'my sister courtesan', or 'my lady') for high-class courtesan the ranks were *yobidashi* or *yobidashi chūsan*, *chūsan* and *tsukemawashi*. Below them came *zashimochi*, *heyamochi* and *shinzō*. Other prostitutes were referred to as *kiri* [short-time], *kashi* [moatside], *shiroku-mise* [4–6 shops — referring to girls whose price dropped from 600 *mon* in the daytime to 400 *mon* for an evening dalliance]. Unlicensed prostitutes, amongst other things, were referred to as 'golden cat', 'silver cat', 'boat tart', 'night hawk' and 'kick-for-a-roll'.

[62] For a fair complexion the help of *Konsei*, the *Shintō* god of childbirth and marriage, who commonly takes the form of a phallus of stone, wood or bronze, was evoked as the God of Whitening. Genchi Katō, 'A Study of Religious Ideas Among the Japanese People as Illustrated by Japanese Phallicism', *Transactions of the Asiatic Society of Japan*, 2nd ser., Supplement to vol.1, 1924, p.10, quoted in U.A. Casal, 'Japanese Cosmetics and Teeth Blackening', *Transactions of the Asiatic Society of Japan*, 3rd ser., Supplement to vol.9, 1966, p.9.

The rising popularity of *geisha* during the early nineteenth century marked a change in the tastes of the Edo populace. At this time illegal bordellos had became numerous and, in order to remain competitive, the Yoshiwara reduced prices and broadened the type of clientele; consequently standards dropped, and courtesans who carried the burden of a greater work load were increasingly maltreated. During the years 1841–1843 the government undertook a number of reforms known as the *Tempō* reforms.[79] As a result, unregulated prostitution was outlawed and illegal prostitutes rounded up and sold to bordellos in the Yoshiwara; their presence further contaminated the standards of the licensed quarters. *Geisha* who restricted their entertaining strictly to music

63 Originally *oshiroi* was made from white soil and rice flour, later a liquid made from the floury seeds of the jalap plant was used. From the seventh century mercury chloride and white lead imported from China and then from Europe were used as the base for a facial powder, but after the toxic qualities of lead became known in the 1870s a lead-free powder was developed. This powder was thinned with water and made into a paste [*neri-oshiroi*] before use. It was sold in wrapped in paper on which appeared portraits of beautiful women or actors. Takahashi Masao et al., *Beni to Oshiroi*, Yokkaichi: Yokkaichi City Museum, 1995, p.12, and Casal, in *Transactions of the Asiatic Society of Japan* (9, 1966), p.9

64 The significance of this combination of colours may be related to their relative purity and impurity in *Shintō* belief. Perhaps the intermingling of the two colours may explain the significance of the modern symbolism of pink as an erotic colour. An unidentified Kyoto *geisha* explains the symbolism of red in J. Cobb, *Geisha,* New York and Toronto: Alfred A. Knopf, 1995, p.74.

65 Women from samurai families shaved off their eyebrows as a sign of reaching full maturity. Commoners kept their eyebrows until the birth of their first child. Drawing in of eyebrows was practised only by prostitutes and unmarried women. After the Meiji period (1868–1912) both teeth blackening and eyebrow drawing were banned. Masao et al., *Beni to Oshiroi* (1995), p.18.

66 In Japan the beauty of perfect teeth was not considered important, as in the West. The custom of a giggling girl covering her mouth with a raised hand so as not to reveal her teeth dates back to Yoshiwara etiquette and, along with teeth blackening, probably relates to the Buddhist notion of white teeth revealing our animal nature. At the beginning of the Edo period, as a sign of developing maturity, girls blackened their teeth from the age of thirteen, later seventeen became the accepted age to begin. In Osaka and Kyoto both male and female court nobles blackened their teeth as did *geisha* and prostitutes. In Edo, only the prostitutes of the Yoshiwara followed this custom. There was also a practical reason for dyeing teeth, for the dye was said to protect the teeth against decay. Casal, in *Transactions of the Asiatic Society of Japan* (9, 1966), p.18, Masao et al., *Beni to Oshiroi* (1995), p.16.

67 The unique nature of the Yoshiwara was emphasised by its own dialect, known as *arinsu* dialect because of its distinctive use of the verb *arimasu* 'be' or 'exist'. The Yoshiwara was also referred to as *arinsu-koku*, or country of the *arinsu* dialect. Seigle, *Yoshiwara: The glittering world of the Japanese courtesan* (1993), p.229–232.

68 Casal, in *Transactions of the Asiatic Society of Japan* (9, 1966), p.24.

69 Hara Budayū, *Tonari no senki* [Intruding Upon Others], 1763. *Enseki jisshu*, vol.5, p.287, quoted in Seigle, *Yoshiwara: The glittering world of the Japanese courtesan* (1993), p.205.

70 The forerunner of the modern day kimono, the *kosode* [small sleeves] was usually worn as an everyday outer garment by all Japanese from about the mid seventeenth century. Its distinctive shape is determined by its relatively simple construction which consists of four rectangular lengths of cloth. Small wrist openings define the *kosode*, whilst those with long hanging sleeves are often referred to as *furisode* [swinging sleeves].

71 In this series Utamaro has drawn on classical tradition, for *Hana-awase* or 'flower matching' was a Heian period aristocratic game in which flowers were matched for their beauty.

72 *Ukiyo-e* artists, living as they did on the periphery of society, empathised with the lives of the courtesans and, when given the opportunity, depicted the same in black and white illustrated novels. Catalogue *Ukiyo-e ni miru Edo no seikatsu* [Edo Life Seen in *ukiyo-e* Prints], Tokyo: Nihon Fūzokushi Gakkai, 1980, pl.90 cited in Seigle, *Yoshiwara: The glittering world of the Japanese courtesan* (1993), p.214.

In a number of frank images from a series showing the lives of prostitutes, Utagawa Toyokuni III (1786–1864) has depicted such taboo subjects as punishment, pregnancy and abortion. Around 1868 Kawanabe Kyōsai (1831–1889) produced a series of eight coloured images showing prostitutes suffering and being cruelly treated by society. For an illustration of one of these prints, see Timothy Clark, *The Art of Kawanabe Kyōsai*, London: British Museum Press, 1993 p.107, cat.67.

73 Venereal diseases were known as 'flower and willow diseases' after the name given to the Yoshiwara. Seigle, *Yoshiwara: The glittering world of the Japanese courtesan* (1993), p.212.

74 In 1899, J.E. de Becker, in his somewhat puritanical study of the Yoshiwara, 'The Nightless City', states that these women, known also as *jigoku*, or *yotaka* [night hawks] were riddled with syphilitic sores and that their noses were eaten away by the disease. These deformities were concealed by a thick layer of white make-up, headscarves, and noses replaced by coloured candle wax. J.E. deBecker, *The Nightless City*, Rutland and Tokyo: Charles E. Tuttle, 1972, pp.326–327. One of the reasons prostitutes painted their fingernails was to disguise the crescents, a traditional indicator of the state of health in Eastern medicine. Casal, in *Transactions of the Asiatic Society of Japan* (9, 1966), p.14.

75 J. Stephenson, *Yoshitoshi's One Hundred Aspects of the Moon*, San Francisco: San Francisco Graphic Society, 1992, p.168.

76 Monica Bethe, 'Reflections on *Beni*: Red as a key to Edo-period fashion', in Dale Carolyn Gluckman and Sharon Sadako Takeda (eds), *When Art became Fashion: Kosode in Edo-period Japan,* New York and Los Angeles: Weatherhill, Inc. and Los Angeles County Museum of Art, 1992. In this essay Bethe discusses the cultural significance of red to the Japanese, particularly the expensive and therefore luxurious *beni*-red. She mentions that, as a means of bypassing the frequent laws banning the use of this colour, red was used for the lining of *kosode* and as a colour for undergarments.

77 T. Clark, *Ukiyo-e Paintings in the British Museum*, London: British Museum Press, 1992, p.17.

78 In the 1680s entertainment was provided by *odoriko* or young teenage dancers also skilled at *shamisen* and singing, later because of their association with prostitution their role was taken over by older women known as *geiko* later also referred to as *geisha*. Seigle, *Yoshiwara: The glittering world of the Japanese courtesan* (1993), pp.171–173.

79 During the Edo period there were three major reforms of which the Tempō reform was one, these were instituted by the Tokugawa government and named after their respective eras. The other two were the Kyōho Reforms (1716–36) and the Kansei Reforms (1787–93). Generally, these reforms were a result of economic adversity, popular unrest or the policy of new political leadership. Part of these reforms was the control and regulation of the production of *ukiyo-e*, and the main areas of concern in this regard were political subversion, sexual impropriety and ostentatious behaviour contrary to Neo-Confucian morality. Under constant threat of prosecution for contravening these laws, the prohibitions and the struggle to skirt around them provided much of the background for the history of *ukiyo-e*. The most famous case of prosecution was that of Utamaro who, in 1804, had designed a triptych entitled *Taiko Gosai Rakuto Yukan no zu* in which he defied government bans by labelling each figure depicted with the actual name of the historical character. For this he was imprisoned and handcuffed for fifty days. See S.E. Thompson, 'The Politics of Japanese Prints', in Dawn Lawson (ed.), *Undercurrents in the Floating World: Censorship and Japanese prints,* New York: The Asia Society Galleries, 1991.

fig.30

BEAUTY & VIOLENCE[80]

The unique nature of Japanese society during the Edo period was buttressed by the official policy of seclusion from the rest of the world [*sakoku*]. For more than 200 years the only Western contact was with Dutch traders who were permitted to operate from the man-made island of Dejima in Nagasaki bay. *Sakoku* lasted until 1854 when Commodore Matthew Perry of the US Navy sailed into Edo bay accompanied by an armed force of sailors and marines in eight warships. Perry carried a letter from the President of the United States of America demanding that Japan open diplomatic and commercial relations. The isolation of the Edo period had come to an end.

Although this incident became a potent symbol of transformation, change was already overtaking feudal Japan. During the early nineteenth century, social and economic problems, along with a growing perception of the West, both stimulated a thirst for Western knowledge and provoked a conservative backlash that rejected 'corruptive foreign influences' — including Neo-Confucianism and Buddhism. Under the slogan 'Revere the Emperor, Expel the Barbarians', native *Shintō* traditions were advanced as the bulwark of a new conservatism. The Tokugawa shogunate's capitulation to foreign pressure was seen as weak and caused a reaction against the government which led to its overthrow in 1868–69 and the restoration of imperial rule under Emperor Meiji (1852–1912). The transference of political power was symbolised on 26 November 1868 when Emperor Meiji travelled from the ancient imperial capital of Kyoto and walked in procession into Edo — now named Tokyo [Eastern Capital]. A policy of modernisation and Westernisation was adopted towards the ideal of 'civilisation and enlightenment', under which the trappings symbolic of samurai power, such as the wearing of swords and hair styled in the traditional topknot, were discouraged and people were urged to adopt Western values and customs. In this climate the Edo period institutions represented by the Yoshiwara *bijin* and the *Kabuki onnagata* appeared as anachronisms.

The popular art of *ukiyo-e* soon reflected changes in taste as well as the apprehension that accompanied social upheaval. Meiji modernisation also led to an interest in prints reflecting Japan's adoption of Western ideas as depicted in contemporary events and fashions.[81] The traditional subjects of courtesans and actors gave way to warrior prints [*musha-e*], often depicting heroes from Chinese and Japanese history, images of the fantastic and the macabre, nature prints and scenic views of famous locales.

The triptych *Edo meisho Tsukiji namiji no yakei* [Night view at the breakwater at Tsukiji, Edo], by Kawanabe Kyōsai (1831–1889), (fig.31) is unusual in its combination of the somewhat outmoded subject of courtesans and a contemporary scene full of colourful local detail.

Tsukiji, near the mouth of the Sumida river, was famous for its fish. In a teahouse overlooking Edo bay three courtesans entertain customers. The woman on the right, whose robe is decorated with fallen maple leaves, is identified by her name cartouche as Omaki from Nakanochō — the central avenue of the Yoshiwara. While she strums a *shamisen* and sings, her two companions dance with fans. The blue ground and designs of their kimono reinforce the nautical theme. One of the dancers, identified as Okoma also from Nakanochō, has a fanciful design of octopuses [*tako*] at play. On her fan, a poem written by the *haiku* poet Ryyōko (Hosojima Seizō) makes the traditional reference to flowers alluding to a woman's beauty:

> It is cherry blossoms that always charm
> A hundred out of a hundred people.

fig.31

The other woman, Okaru from the Iwai-ya bordello, wears a kimono with the image of a carp [*koi*] swimming upstream, a traditional symbol of courage and perseverance. In this festive atmosphere both motifs are apt, for the words *tako* and *koi*, with different Chinese characters, can be read as 'great happiness' and 'love'. On the *obi* of the third woman, the image of Raijin the god of thunder, a good omen, is cavorting amongst clouds.

An innovative element is the use of the newly imported Prussian blue; here, overprinted with black in the sky, its use effectively suggests depth. Prussian blue led the vanguard of the synthetic aniline dyes that were imported into Japan during the first half of the nineteenth century, replacing the delicate traditional organic pigments and adding a brilliant intensity to prints[82] — a change that was indicative of the emerging taste for what was perceived as 'modern' and 'Western'.

As a symbol of Westernisation, Tsukiji itself became famous, for four years after this print was produced the first official government guest house, the Tsukiji Hotel, was built there in a 'Western style'.

fig.32

The lifting of restrictions on travel within Japan at the beginning of the nineteenth century resulted in a heightened interest in the traditional subject of landscape prints, with human content an important element, but shown as participants rather than the principal element.[83] Hiroshige's scenes in and around Edo epitomise this genre.

In the series *Tōkaidō gojūsan tsui* [Fifty-three Parallels for the Tōkaidō Highway], Utagawa Kuniyoshi (1797–1861) has taken up a theme introduced by Hiroshige in his series of the most important communication link between Edo and Kyoto ('Fifty-three Stages of the Tōkaidō Highway', *c.*1833–34). Unlike the conventional staffage found in Hiroshige's scenes however, Kuniyoshi, in a print from his series, has highlighted an *ukiyo-e*-style local beauty — an abalone fisherwoman. (fig.32) The image of a beautiful woman has been used to advertise the pleasures of the location, Yui, in the province of Tōtōmi. One of the stations along the Tōkaidō, Yui was famous for its seafood and for the view it afforded of Mount Fuji and the pine trees along Miho beach.

Here the commercial reality of *ukiyo-e* is plain to see. Within the unusual crustacean-shaped cartouche of this print the text extols the attractions of Yui and the speciality of the local teahouse — where they cook and serve the best abalone and other shellfish. The tradition of *ukiyo-e* as a promoter of popular fashion is maintained with the woman wearing a Japanese robe of a popular indigo tie-dyed fabric. *Ukiyo-e* artists such as Hiroshige and Utamaro also produced prints highlighting this particular cloth.

During the turbulent changes of the early nineteenth century, the depiction of figures from the distant past included heroic women. Around 1841 Kuniyoshi produced a series of prints, *Kenjo Reppuden* [Stories of Wise Women and Faithful Wives]. Strong independent women as warriors had been depicted in early *ukiyo-e* and their stories were revived as models for the nation to follow — although not for women in their ordinary lives. In a print from the series, Kuniyoshi has taken as his subject the story of the widow Oiko.[84] (fig.33)

fig.33

Oiko lived in Takashima, near Lake Biwa, in Omi province (present day Shiga prefecture). The local villagers despised her and prevented water from flowing into her rice paddies. One night Oiko dammed the mouth of the village irrigation channel with a huge rock measuring about two metres in diameter. At dawn the villagers were surprised to see the rock, and with great effort several of them tried to remove it, but failed. Feeling remorse they apologised profusely to Oiko who then removed it with no effort. The story of her incredible strength became so legendary that a rock at the site was named 'Oiko's channel mouth rock'. Both Hokusai and, later, Yoshitoshi produced prints illustrating the unbelievable strength of Oiko.[85]

fig.34

Inspired by his teacher, Kuniyoshi's work, Tsukioka Yoshitoshi (1839–1892) depicted a scene from the Kabuki play *Osanago no Adachi* [A Child's Revenge] — *Seppu no rei taki ni kakaru zu* [The good woman's spirit praying in the waterfall]. (fig.35)

The play deals with the revenge of Botoru, the son of the samurai Tamiya Genpachiro who had been killed by his jealous rival, Hori Gentazaemon. In order to protect himself, Gentazaemon tricked Botoru into going to a remote village where he planned to kill him too. Botoru's nurse, Otsuji, being aware of the planned ambush but unable to warn Botoru, prayed for his safety.

Yoshitoshi shows the faithful nurse following the traditional austerity of prayer under the cold blast of a waterfall. Otsuji's self-mortification was successful and Botoru was saved, but at the cost of Otsuji's life. Botoru went on to extract his revenge eventually killing Gentazaemon.

The tradition of dutiful and self-sacrificing wives carried over into the newly emerging modern Japan, and in another print from Stories of Wise Women and Faithful Wives, the devotions of Hatsuhana, wife of Inuma Katsugorō, are lauded. (fig.34)

Whilst in pursuit of the man who had killed his father, Katsugorō injured his knee. Hatsuhana carried her crippled husband up to the sacred Gongen waterfall at Hakone. There, for a hundred days under the cascade of the waterfall, she prayed to the deity of Hakone-gongen for Katsugorō's recovery. Finally cured of his lameness, Katsugorō killed his father's murderer, who was passing by — too late to save Hatsuhana who had already been murdered by her husband's enemies.

Meditating under an icy-cold waterfall was an austerity practised by monks as a means of focusing their devotion. Kuniyoshi depicts Hatsuhana at prayer under the waterfall, her hands clasped fervently and her toes curled as she endures the cold blast of water spraying over her in a spectacular display.

fig.35

In an effort to suppress any dissension throughout the Edo period, the Tokugawa authorities had banned the depiction of contemporary events. The Meiji government lifted this ban and prints of current events were produced, usually in a sensational manner. Yoshitoshi was the first artist to depict the drama surrounding the Meiji Restoration. Having witnessed the bloody overthrow of the Tokugawa shogunate, and the subsequent betrayal of the samurai who had supported the Meiji reforms, Yoshitoshi was particularly sympathetic to their later rebellion against these same reforms.

In a print from his 1880 series *Azuma-e sugata retsujo kurabe* [Eastern Pictures of Heroic Women Compared], Yoshitoshi's subject is shown in a pose of stoic defiance. (see fig.30) She was the wife of Kirino Toshiaki, a friend and adviser of Saigō Takamori (1826–1877), the leader of the revolt of 1877 known as the Satsuma Rebellion. After their mistreatment by the government, Saigō and Kirino had returned to their province where, under the guise of running a private school, they amassed an army of 40,000 'pupils'. Leading their army they challenged the authority of the government in a campaign known as the *Seinan no Eki* [Southwestern campaign], but the rebellion was quashed and both leaders killed.

Yoshitoshi produced many prints on the theme of the rebellion. His image of Kirino's wife, who led the women support troops, includes the text of a contemporary writer, Danryūrō Enshi, who reports that 'she bravely stood at the head of the women's troops. At the truce she offered help and shared her food with starving soldiers. Participating in the joys and sorrows of the soldiers in the battle field she did her best to help them'. Her resolute expression and clasped hands emphasise determination, as does the restrained colour and design of her robe with its scarlet sleeves into which she cried, 'grieving for her departed husband'. Her stern posture, reinforced by the gnarled nature of the stacked faggots behind, contrasts with the underlying eroticism apparent in all Yoshitoshi's portraits of women — here eloquently expressed in the clear whiteness of her exposed chest, the long sweeping curve of her vulnerable neck, and her dishevelled hair.

In the late Edo period, violent eroticism had been depicted in the works of Utamaro and Hokusai where a rape scene or grotesque images lampooning foreigners had become standard for certain *shunga* series.[86] The violence seen in Yoshitoshi's images is more psychologically disturbing. His unstable personality (he died insane), an extremely chauvinistic attitude toward women, coupled with his vehement reaction to modernisation and the erosion of tradition, expressed itself in brutal images of women that are particularly shocking and also disturbing because of the beauty of their composition and technique.

The subjects for these works were often contemporary events which, by the 1870s, were being published in newspapers. Although colour woodblock prints were considered unsuitable for these publications, special single sheet prints known as 'newspaper prints' sometimes appeared as newspaper supplements. Yoshitoshi exploited this new freedom. In one of a series of twenty pictures published in 1887 as a supplement to the *Yamato Shimbun*, he has depicted an image of 'Old Lady' Muraoka of the Konoe clan bound with a rope. (fig.36)

fig.36

This print refers back to a purge by the Tokugawa authorities of political leaders and court nobles who opposed the government's policies. The uprising that initiated the purge was a reaction to the government's signing, in 1858, of commercial trade treaties with foreign countries. Known as the Ansei Purge, the action resulted in many of the leaders of the uprising being executed and others being transported to Edo in cages. Among those arrested was 'Old Lady' Muraoka of the Konoe clan.

The text reports that Tsuzaki Noriko (1786–1873), or Lady Muraoka, was a sentimental patriot who deplored the undermining of the court's authority by the shogunate. She was arrested and interrogated for many days, but did not show any signs of submission. Instead she spoke of the political failures of the shogunate, filling her inquisitors with dismay. In a mixture of beauty, sensuality and violence, Yoshitoshi has depicted Lady Muraoka, beautifully dressed and sporting an aristocratic hairstyle and make-up. The rope binding accentuates the vulnerability of her neck and disarray of her costume as she bites down heavily on a loose strand of hair, a common convention in erotic images.

The aspirations and desires of the Edo period *chōnin* had placed the courtesan of high rank on a pedestal as an ideal of female beauty. Changing times required a different model and, by the Meiji period, women defending traditional values were elevated to the status of heroine. In a characteristically Japanese contradiction, women were also regarded as impure and, for this reason, inferior to men. Their sexuality, seen also as demonic, was a corrupting influence. On the one hand Yoshitoshi exorcised these demons by depicting women as scapegoats, being murdered or brutalised, but he also represented women as being in possession of supernatural powers. In a work from the series *Shinkei sanjurokkaisen* [New Forms of Thirty-six Ghosts], a rural beauty dressed in luxurious attire more appropriate to a Yoshiwara courtesan, reveals her demonic nature. (fig.37)

The subject is Kiyohime, the daughter of an innkeeper of Masago village. The inn was on the route to Kumano shrine. Anchin, a pious monk of Dōjō temple on the banks of the Hidaka river, lodged at the inn on his annual pilgrimages

fig.37

to the shrine. Over the years Kiyohime became attracted to Anchin, and as a grown woman she declared her love for him. Dismayed by her passion, Anchin fled back to his temple. In pursuit, Kiyohime was blocked by the Hidaka river in flood. Her vindictiveness changed her into a serpent, enabling her to swim across the river. Anchin hid under a large bronze bell in the grounds of the temple, but Kiyohime, still in the form of a serpent, found him out and coiled herself around the bell. The heat of her anger caused the bell to melt, killing both of them.

Yoshitoshi has depicted Kiyohime, partially metamorphosed, emerging from the river. The pattern of scales on her robe and the bold bands on her trailing cloak emphasise her serpentine nature. The blood-red of her underrobe adds to the highly-charged emotion of the print, for in Japan red is closely connected with curses.

Yoshitoshi stands alone in his treatment of traditional subject matter which he continued to feature in later works as he joined his friend, the *Kabuki* actor Ichikawa Danjuro IX, in a move to revive past traditions.[87]

Sustained peace, a rigidly structured society, and enforced isolation from the outside world, characterised the Edo period. In this environment an economically powerful merchant class [*chōnin*] emerged. Although they were denied political power, wealth allowed the *chōnin* to overcome class barriers and to emerge as the cultural elite. Theirs was a popular culture, fashioned around the pursuit of pleasure. They delighted in beauty — both the ephemeral beauty found in nature and the stylised ideal of beauty of the high-ranking courtesans, celebrated in paintings and prints, and impersonated on the *Kabuki* stage.

The images produced in the rarefied atmosphere of this isolated society reflect the preoccupations of the populace; they reveal an evolution in taste for depictions of female beauty and fashion during the Edo period. The early, understated seventeenth-century Kambun beauty, by the eighteenth century had been replaced by the high-ranking courtesan whose costume and make-up eventually became so ostentatious that she was unrecognisable as a real woman. Her degeneration into this state, lamented by contemporary writers, heightened the popularity of the cultivated beauty and refined skills of the *geisha* and led ultimately to the demise of the Yoshiwara licensed pleasure quarters.

The social and political upheaval that overtook nineteenth-century Japan provoked a change in artistic taste and direction that would further relegate the Yoshiwara beauty to the distant past. However, images of these women, characterised by an earthy humour and a highly refined artistic expression, remain as indelible evocations of beauty and desire, frozen in time.

Notes continued: pages 37–43

80 Inspired by John Stevenson intro., 'Beauty & Violence', *Society for Japanese Arts*, Eindhon, The Netherlands: Havilland Press, 1992.

81 This fascination gave rise to *ukiyo-e* known as *Yokohama-e* [Yokohama prints], after the port of Yokohama (opened in 1859), depicting the foreigners who used this port.

82 Referred to by the Edo period Japanese as *bero*, after Berlin where it was first manufactured in 1704; the first recorded use of Prussian blue in the Japanese visual arts was 1778. It was not introduced into Japanese printmaking until the early 1830s and was influential in the increased interest in landscape prints, especially those of Hokusai and Hiroshige during this period.

83 The interest in landscape itself as a subject matter was deeply established in Japanese painting and part of this tradition were landscapes showing views of the most famous sites of one or more of the provinces (*mesho-e*).

84 This story is based on a collection of folk tales, *Kokan Chomon-shu*, compiled by Tachibana Narisue in 1254. James A. Michener, *The Hokusai Sketch-books: Selections from the manga*, Tokyo: Charles E. Tuttle, 1979, p. 186–187.

85 Hokusai, in his *Manga* of 1814, and Yoshitoshi, in a diptych of 1889, depicted the story of how Oiko held captive the great warrior Saeki Ujinaga by clamping his wrist under her armpit

86 Utamaro's famous *shunga* series, *Utamakura* [Poem of the pillow] 1788 contains three images of a disturbing or exotic nature. In one, an abalone diver is raped underwater by *kappa*, grotesque mythological river-monsters. In another, a girl is raped by a hairy old man. Another is a hideous representation of an elderly Dutch couple. In 1814 Hokusai produced his famous image of a diving-girl being violated by octopuses in his series *Kinoe no komatsu* [Pining for love].

87 The National Gallery of Australia has in its collection a triptych by Yoshitoshi, *Ichikawa Danjuro IX* (as Musashiro Benkei in *Kanjincho*), purchased 1995, depicting the famous actor in a role based on events surrounding the Taira/Minamoto wars of twelfth-century Japan.

Nishikawa SUKENOBU

Kyoto 1671–1750
Girl with koto
after *c.*1717
Artist's signature: *Yamato eshi Nishikawa Sukenobu hitsu* [Painted by the Japanese-style artist Nishikawa Sukenobu]
chūban sumizuri-e, monochrome woodblock print
26.2 x 17.9 cm
Collection: The Art Gallery of New South Wales
Purchased 1930

The *koto,* a thirteen-stringed semi-cylindrical zither, is laid on the floor to be played by a performer in a kneeling position who plucks the strings with three ivory picks attached to the fingers. An early form of the *koto* was used in court music of the Nara period (710–794). By the fifteenth century the *koto* was being played as a solo instrument as well as accompanying other instruments and voices. In the seventeenth century the *koto* was played in ensemble with the *shamisen* and a long-necked bowed lute, the *kokū.* This type of ensemble playing became a popular form of entertainment in private homes as well as in the licensed pleasure quarters.

Before the development of a method of printing in full colour, by accurately aligning the several sheets that correspond to the various colours of an image, prints such as this were produced by a single impression in black ink [*sumi*]. Sometimes colour was added by brush.

In his design for this monochrome print of a young woman carrying a *koto* Sukenobu has paid particular attention to details of her costume and the treatment of her hair. Such elements, reflecting the cultivated tastes of the period, would soon be given full expression in brilliant colour. (See 'Nishiki-e', pages 9–11.)

44

大和繪師 西川祐信筆

Plate 2

45

Suzuki HARUNOBU

Edo 1724–1770
A courtesan writing a love letter
late 1760s
Artist's signature: *Harunobu ga*
hashira-e, colour woodblock print
66.2 x 12.4 cm

National Gallery of Victoria, Felton Bequest, 1909

The long, narrow format of the pillar print
[*hashira-e*] was used to great effect by Harunobu
and later by Utamaro. The technique of cropping
the figures in effect gives a partial view, or a more
intimate glimpse into the private lives of the
courtesans. In this image we share the view
of a courtesan writing a letter with the two men
who peer through the window. The hooded man
holding a fan carefully conceals his identity.
The inscription on the fan by the poet Sashin reads:

Spring, autumn coloured moon.

The significant achievement of designing the
earliest full colour prints is often attributed
to Harunobu. (See pages 9–11.)

Isoda KORYUSAI

Edo active *c.*1764–88
Matsukaze dancing
beneath the robe of the courtier Yukihira
*c.*1770
Artist's signature: *Koryūsai ga*
hashira-e, colour woodblock print
69.7 x 12.8 cm

National Gallery of Victoria, Felton Bequest, 1909

This print illustrates one of the principal characters
in a Heian period story of love betrayed.
(See pages 13–14.) The location is Suma, famous
for its pine trees.

The long 'swinging sleeves' of Matsukaze's robe
[*furisode*] symbolise her youth (this style was usually
worn by young girls under the age of nineteen).
The delicate design of drooping willows is
especially suited to this type of costume for the
slender, graceful shape of the willow was considered
to be feminine in nature and often appears in
Japanese literature as a metaphor for feminine
beauty — in this design perhaps as a counterpoint
to the pine tree above, a symbol of masculinity.

Plate 3

Plate 4

Nishikawa SUKENOBU

Kyoto 1671–1750
Standing beauty [*Tachi bijin*]
1736–1748
Artist's signature: *Nishikawa Ukyō Sukenobu hitsu*
[Painted by Nishikawa Sukenobu of Ukyō rank]
Seal: *Nishikawa-uji, Sukenobu kore* [*o*] *zu* [*su*]
[This was drawn by Sukenobu]
hanging scroll [*kakemono*], ink and colour
on silk
78.0 x 30.0 cm
Klaus F. Naumann Collection

The slightly dishevelled appearance of this young courtesan contrasts with the apparent innocence of her expression. Her outer robe, decorated with a pattern of grape vines on a green ground, hangs loosely from her shoulders revealing a scarlet robe beneath decorated with flowering bush clover [*hagi*]. Red, especially in contrast with the purity of a white underrobe or pale skin, was considered especially alluring. The bush clover, representative of autumn and the autumn colours of grape leaves — here partly rendered using a tie-dye technique — evoke a mood of melancholy which is reflected in the girl's beautiful, sad face.

The refinement of Sukenobu's images of beautiful young women was characteristic of the Kyoto *ukiyo-e* school, of which he was a leading figure. This prolific and influential artist illustrated novels and produced picture books, including albums of *shunga*. He also illustrated several volumes of kimono design — Sukenobu's interest in design is reflected in his realistic depiction of costume.

Plate 5

Katsukawa SHUNSHO

Edo active *c*.1726–93
Standing beauty [*Tachi bijin*]
c.1789–92
Artist's signature: *Katsu Shunshō ga*
hanging scroll [*kakemono*], ink and colour
on silk
85.8 x 34.0 cm
Klaus F. Naumann Collection

Shunshō was a popular designer of actor prints —
one of the major subjects of *ukiyo-e*. Late in his
career he painted portraits of beautiful
sophisticated women: this particular tall, willowy
beauty is a characteristic example. Both her outer
robe and underrobe are decorated at the hems with
a bold, masculine checked pattern. In contrast,
her *obi* is delicately decorated with a floral design
in gold thread. These sexually ambiguous
associations would have been considered erotic.

Whilst adjusting her hairpin, the woman appears
to have been disturbed by some action beyond the
picture frame. She leans back elegantly to look over
her shoulder — perhaps her lover has entered the
room. In her left hand she holds a letter, another
element that allows the viewer to speculate about
the romantic nature of the image.

Plate 6

Torii KIYONAGA

Edo 1752–1815
Salt-maidens
1783
Artist's signature: *Kiyonaga ga*
Publisher: *Nishimura-ya*
hashira-e, colour woodblock print
66.7 x 10.2 cm
Collection: The Art Gallery of New South Wales
Purchased 1952

Two women are gathering brine for salt making. This may be a scene from the medieval *Nō* play *Matsukaze*. (See pages 13–14.) Rather than the traditional setting of the play, Suma, the location depicted here would be more familiar to the citizens of Edo — Tagonoura on the coast of central Honshū, an area celebrated in ancient poems and famous for its views of Mount Fuji, seen in the background.

Torii KIYONAGA

Edo 1752–1815
Courtesan and her attendant at the New Year
1785
Artist's signature: *Kiyonaga ga*
Publisher: *Nishimura-ya*
hashira-e, colour woodblock print
64.2 x 11.6 cm
National Gallery of Victoria, Felton Bequest, 1909

A high ranking courtesan and her child trainee [*kamuro*] shelter under the eaves of a building. It is New Year, the most elaborate of Japan's annual festivals, and preparations have been made to welcome Toshigami, the deity of the coming year. A sacred rope of straw with hanging white paper strips [*shide*] that serve to attract the gods has been hung under the eaves to indicate the temporary home of the deity and protect it from malevolent spirits. The traditional New Year decorations of pine, bamboo and plum are strung around the eaves. The evergreen pine and bamboo, and the plum — the first tree to bloom in spring — collectively have been regarded in China and Japan as the symbol of hope and good fortune. The two women may have just returned from a visit to a shrine for the young *kamuro* is admiring a battledore (a racket used in shuttlecock) bought at shrines as talismans to bring luck for the year.

Torii KIYONAGA

Edo 1752–1815
Hand-basin
1787
Artist's signature: *Kiyonaga ga*
kakemono-e, colour woodblock print
86.0 x 38.0 cm
Collection: Queensland Art Gallery, Queensland Art Gallery Society

The courtesan at the hand-basin prepares to wash herself. The wad of tissue she holds in her mouth — *onkotogami* [paper for the honourable act] — suggests that her patron has just departed. The sleeve of her costume bears her individual crest [*mon*]. Patrons would have been able to identify her by consulting books such as the *Kamon-zukushi* [Collected House Crests] — crests of Yoshiwara courtesans. The courtesan on the verandah sits provocatively with one knee raised, talking to a man whose form can seen through the translucent paper of the sliding door [*shōji*].

Plate 7

Plate 8

Plate 9

Kitagawa UTAMARO

Edo 1753–1806
Hairdressing [*Kami-yui*]
from the series *Twelve Types of Women's
Handicraft* [*Fujin tewaza jūni-kō*] c.1798–99
Artist's signature: *Utamaro hitsu*
Publisher: *Wakayasa Yoichi*
ōban, colour woodblock print
38.1 x 26.7 cm
Art Gallery of South Australia, Adelaide,
South Australian Government Grant 1983

A hairdresser is carefully combing her client's hair in preparation for creating an elaborate style. Internal supports were used to build the fantastic shapes that characterised Edo period hairstyles, so complex in the eighteenth century that the skills of a professional hairdresser were required — thus the occupation developed and was practised in salons or privately in residences.

A courtesan's hair, although washed only once a month, was cleaned daily using a fine-tooth comb and perfumed oil — a pomade made from aloe-wood oil. So as not to disturb her coiffure when resting, a special lacquered headrest was used which was perforated at the top and along the sides to allow fumes from incense placed in a special drawer underneath to perfume the hair.

The rendering of fine details such as eyes and hair in *ukiyo-e* often required a number of separate blocks and the skills of a specialised wood engraver. In this work particular attention has been paid to the strands of hair being drawn through the comb, each separately delineated.

Plate 10

Kitagawa UTAMARO

Edo 1753–1806

Two women

*c.*1798–99

Artist's signature: *Utamaro hitsu*

Publisher: *Omiya Gonkurō*

ôban, colour woodblock print with mica

38.1 x 25.4 cm

Los Angeles County Museum of Art,

Gift of Frederick Weisman Company

The young woman in the foreground bends over to grate radish [*daikon*] for the dish she is preparing and, in doing so, reveals her delicate white breast. Her firm grip on the radish is an erotic reference that would not have been overlooked by a public alert to visual puns in *ukiyo-e* — 'large root' [*daikon*] and 'male root' [*dankon*] both share the same Chinese character.

The girl's companion has shaved eyebrows and blackened teeth — characteristics that indicate her maturity. The permanence of the colour black, made by the oxidation of a mixture of iron or nails soaked in tea and *sake*, symbolised the fidelity of a married woman whose loyalty to her husband remained as constant and deep as this pigment.

The women appear to belong to the samurai class for they are both wearing their hair in a style popular with that class — tied high at the back to give an imposing appearance.

This print is from a series of eleven known designs published over a period of three to four years, depicting women involved in various household activities.

Plate 11

Chōkōsai EISHO

Edo active 1780–1800
Eizan of the Take-ya brothel [*Take-ya Eizan*]
*c.*1795–96
Artist's signature: *Eishō ga*
Publisher: *Yamaguchi-ya*
ōban, colour woodblock print
38.7 x 26.3 cm
Art Gallery of South Australia, Adelaide,
South Australian Government Grant 1984

Until the sixteenth century Japanese women wore their long hair untied, then *Kabuki* actresses and courtesans began to fashion their hair in styles similar to those worn by men. During the Edo period women's hairstyles became more complex and incorporated decorative haircombs and hairpins made from lacquered wood, tortoiseshell or metal.

In this print Eisho shows all the elements that distinguished the coiffure of a high ranking courtesan — the hair is divided into four sections: forelock, side locks, back hair, and topknot — then tied to make a puff at the back. The side locks were also tied and supported by a piece of metal or bone so that these parts of the hair would protrude. Finally the forelock and topknot were bound. The topknot was tied at its base using a cord of tightly rolled paper, the more strands used the higher the topknot.

In *ukiyo–e* pictures of beautiful women, hair style was an important element; its delineation required the virtuoso skills of specialised wood engravers. Numerous blocks were used to print the hair, each adding further depth and detail.

竹屋内 紫尽山

栄昌画

Plate 12

Plate 13

Kitagawa UTAMARO
Edo 1753–1806
Four-armed scoop-net [*Yotsude-ami*]
*c.*1800–01
Artist's signature: *Utamaro hitsu*
Censor's seal: *kiwame*
ōban triptych, colour woodblock print,
37.5 x 74.8 cm
National Gallery of Australia

Utamaro's print designs are renowned for their strong compositions and innovative visual effects. In this triptych he has employed the crossed arms of the scoop-net of the fishing boat to link effectively the three sheets of the triptych. Perspective is suggested by the overprinting of the net, subtly rendered in brown ink.

While revellers and courtesans cavort in the pleasure boat [*yakatabune*], one woman tries to distract the fisherman with the offer of a drink of *sake*. Two others have boarded the fishing boat to inspect the catch.

This scene of two young dandies accompanied by seven beauties would have excited male interest, but in reality outings such as this, where entertainment and food were enjoyed in a scenic locale, were more balanced affairs.

Plate 14

Keisai EISEN

Edo 1790–1848
Woman with umbrella
*c.*1820s
Artist's signature: *Keisai Eisen ga*
Publisher: *Matsumoto Sahei*
Censor's seal: *kiwame*
kakemono-e, colour woodblock print
71.0 x 24.0 cm
ANU Art Collection

A young woman caught in a snowfall is struggling to open her umbrella Her feet in their wooden clogs [*geta*] are fashionably bare despite the cold, although her toes are curled over — a common *ukiyo-e* convention to show the unleashing of passionate emotions.

The hems of her outer robe and underrobe feature designs of flowering grasses and maple leaves. The overall green colour is softly graded, the darker tones highlighting the flakes of snow — spots of unprinted paper. The roses on her padded jacket are placed where family crests would normally have been seen.

On her black *obi* there is a design of bats, repeated as an ornament on her hair pin. Bats were considered a symbol of good luck because the characters for both 'bat' and 'happiness' have the same pronunciation.

The characteristic S-shaped pose elegantly fills the vertical format of this print. The cropping of the image gives the immediacy of a view perhaps glimpsed through the frames of a partly opened screen.

Utagawa KUNIYASU

Edo 1794–1832
Woman with umbrella
c.1820s
Artist's signature: *Kuniyasu ga*
Publisher: *Omi-ya Heihachi*
Censor's seal: *kiwame*
kakemono-e, colour woodblock print
72.3 x 24.8 cm
National Gallery of Australia

Images of women that show glimpses of flesh were known as 'dangerous pictures' [*abuna-e*]. They emerged as a reaction to government bans on the explicitly erotic *shunga*, and were the first works in Japanese art to look at the human body as a subject.

There are obvious sexual connotations in this woman's struggle to maintain decorum whilst firmly gripping the umbrella handle and holding the skirts of her robe high. The artist accentuates this mood by revealing her inner thigh framed by the agitated folds of her undergarment.

Plate 15

61

Kikugawa EIZAN

Edo 1787–1867

A beauty from Seki temple [*Sekidera Komachi*]

from the series *Seven Elegant Beauties*

[*Fūryū nana Komachi*]

*c.*1820s

Artist's signature: *Kikugawa Eizan hitsu*

Publisher: *Izumi-ya Ichibei*

Censor's seal: *kiwame*

ōban, colour woodblock print

38.4 x 25.6 cm

Art Gallery of Western Australia

Purchased 1972

Like Utamaro before him, in this series Eizan has parodied the seven famous events in the life of the female poet Ono no Komachi — one of Japan's six legendary poets [*Rokkasen*] who lived in the ninth century. Komachi was famous for her beauty, wit and passion. Later her name was used as a suffix to place names — referring to an especially beautiful woman of a particular locality.

Here a beauty from Seki temple is looking at her image in two mirrors as she ponders the passage of time and the transience of beauty. Her thoughts translate as:

> May years pass by
> Without my face changing,
> Even though life is not endless

Plate 16

Plate 17

Keisai EISEN

Edo 1790–1848
Woman in kimono with vertical stripes
*c.*1840s
Artist's signature: *Keisai Eisen ga*
kakemono-e, colour woodblock print
69.5 x 23.0 cm
Collection: The Art Gallery of New South Wales
Bequest of Kenneth Myer 1993

Eisen specialised in portraits of beautiful women [*bijin-ga*] especially in the vertical format. His women were characterised by their short stature, thickset necks, and rounded shoulders. This woman's plain robe with bold vertical stripes was a style recommended by contemporary journals on fashion and etiquette as a means of creating the impression of height.

As the woman steps forward she lifts the skirts of her robe, thereby revealing her bare feet. A fully fledged courtesan was forbidden to wear socks, her exposed feet being seen as alluring. Prepared for any sexual encounter, she has tucked into her *obi* an obligatory wad of tissue.

This mannerist image reflects the decadence of the late Edo period.

Keisai EISEN

Edo 1790–1848
A woman going to nagauta lessons
1843–48
Artist's signature: *Keisai Eisen ga*
Publisher: *Sanoki*
Censor's seal: *nanushi*
kakemono-e, colour woodblock print
73.0 x 24.7 cm
Art Gallery of Western Australia
Purchased 1973

The young woman clutching an umbrella holds a song book under her arm — possibly a *nagauta* [long song] book, a type of lyrical song accompanied by the *shamisen* performed in the *Kabuki* theatre and at concerts.

Her kimono is decorated with crests used in an incense identification game — a cultured accomplishment and a difficult task as there were as many as 2,500 types of fragrances. Known as *Genji-kō* crests, these designs were based on the vent pattern of incense burners. Their individual patterns were also used as markers for each of the 54 chapters of the eleventh-century *Tale of Genji*.

Her relatively simple hairstyle indicates that she may be an apprentice *geisha* or a young maiden from a well-to-do family. There is an element of titillation in her slightly dishevelled coiffure, glimpses of her ankle and her exposed neck with a tuft of downy hair.

Plate 18

65

Utagawa KUNISADA I
(TOYOKUNI III)
Edo 1786–1864

*A female Daruma, between Yoshiwara and
Kanbara* [*Yoshiwara Kanbara kan: onna Daruma*]
from the series *Eastern Seaboard Highway*
[*Tōkaidō*]
1852
Artist's signature: *Toyokuni ga*
Publisher: *Tamaya Sōkichi (?)*
ōban , colour woodblock print
35.4 x 24.6 cm
Collection: The Art Gallery of New South Wales
Purchased 1995

Bodhidharma, or *Daruma* in Japanese, is the
legendary founder of Zen Buddhism. Early in the
sixth century he is said to have travelled from
India to China and later to the Shaolin temple
in northern China where he meditated for nine
years whilst facing a wall. In *ukiyo-e* his austerities
are often compared to those of the courtesans
who were contracted to brothels for ten years.
An eighteenth-century poet reflects:

> what are nine years?
> ten years in the suffering world
> dressed in a flowering robe.

Yoshiwara was the licensed brothel district
of Edo; and Kanbara was a station along the
Tōkaidō — the highway that connected Edo and
Kyoto along the eastern seaboard. The cartouche
identifies this town as Iwabuchi, located on the
highway. Kunisada may have used this image
of a courtesan dressed as *Daruma* as a device to
advertise the attractions of Iwabuchi —
emphasising the commercial nature of *ukiyo-e.*

Plate 19

Tsukioka YOSHITOSHI

Tokyo 1839–1892

The old demon woman retrieving her arm
[*Rōba kiwan o mochisaru zu*]
from the series *New Forms of Thirty-six Ghosts*
[*Shinkei sanjurokkaisen*]
1889
Artist's signature: *Yoshitoshi* (and artist's seal)
Publisher: *Sasaki Toyokichi*
Engraver: *Chokuzan*
ōban, colour woodblock print
37.0 x 24.7 cm
National Gallery of Victoria,
Purchased through The Art Foundation of Victoria
with the assistance of Coles Myer

Watanabe no Tsuna (953–1024) was one of the retainers of Minamoto no Yorimitsu (948–1021) who, during the tenth century, waged a battle to rid Japan of demons. Hearing that his master's work had not been completed and that a demon still lived near Rashōmon gate in Kyoto, where it assaulted people and animals, Watanabe went there to investigate. That evening whilst sleeping he was disturbed by the approach of a demon. Lashing out with his sword, he sliced off the creature's arm as it tried to escape. He placed the arm in a casket over which he vowed to recite Buddhist sutras for seven days. On the sixth day he was visited by his aunt — actually the demon in disguise. She inquired about the arm and entreated him to show it to her. When he opened the casket she assumed her true form and, seizing her arm, fled.

Yoshitoshi has depicted the demon fleeing, as she does so her colourful outer robe slips off to reveal her ghostly form. Already the face of the aunt is metamorphosing into the demon Hannya, with its open mouth, sharp fangs and horns; her feet have reverted to characteristic demon's claws. In her left hand she clasps the gnarled form of her severed arm.

This story formed the basis for the *Nō* play *Rashōmon* and the *Kabuki* play *Ibaraki*.

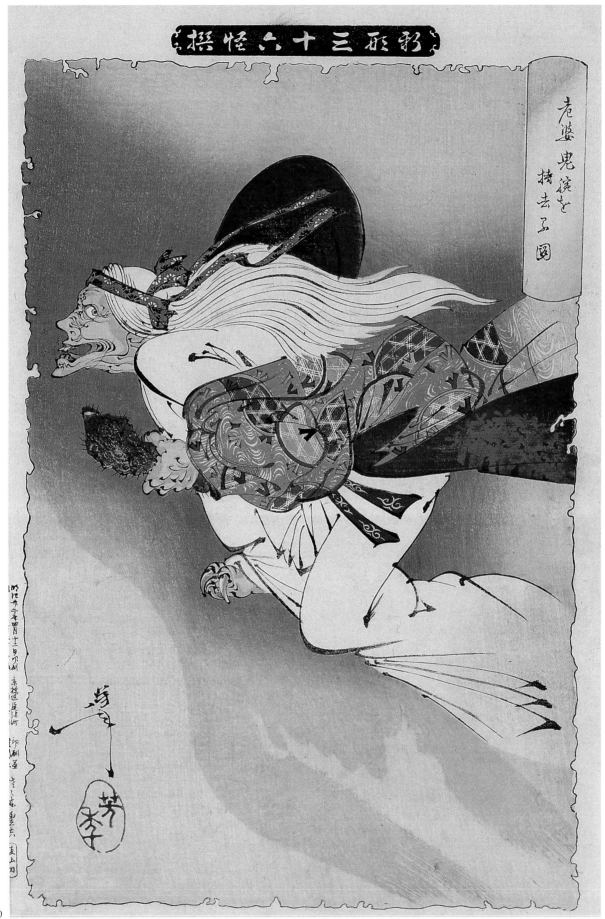

Plate 20

LIST OF ILLUSTRATIONS

All measurements are in centimetres, height before width.
Note that sometimes prints are made in the horizontal format
[*yokoban*]. Hanging scroll and screen measurements refer
to image size. Where identified, the publisher, engraver
and censor's seal have been noted. The traditional format
sizes are cited in the glossary and are only approximate.

LIST OF PLATES

Full caption details accompany the Plates.

GLOSSARY

abuna-e	'dangerous pictures', mildly erotic *ukiyo-e*
aratame	the government censorship seal appearing on prints from 1848
asobi	play, pleasure, amusement
bakufu	military government of the *shōgun* in Edo
bijin	although *bijin* is usually translated as 'beautiful woman' the word is not gender specific, the suffix *jin* meaning person
bijin-ga	pictures which portray 'beautiful women'
chōnin	the townspeople of Edo
chūban	print format measuring 29.0 x 22.0 cm
-e	a suffix meaning picture
furisode	'swinging sleeves', a long-sleeved kimono worn by young, unmarried women and entertainers
-ga	a picture, or 'drawn by', when used as a suffix to artists' signatures
hanga	a woodblock print
hashira-e	a vertical format print known as a 'pillar print' measuring 77.0 x 13.0 cm
hitsu	'brush of', 'drawn by', in artists' signatures
hosoban	print format measuring 33.0 x 15.0 cm
iki	urbane, sophisticated, a sense of refinement — in visual terms *iki* expressed itself in a chic beauty whose sensuality never crossed the boundaries of taste
kakemono	a hanging scroll
kakemono-e	a vertical *ōban* diptych sometimes referred to as a 'hanging scroll' print measuring 76.0 x 23.0 cm
kimono	'thing to wear', a general term for clothing since the late 1800s
kiwame	censors' seals, approval seal which appeared on prints from about 1790 to 1842
kosode	literally 'small sleeve', referring to the size of the wrist opening, also a general term for full length garments made during the Edo period
mie	a dramatic pose in *Kabuki*
mitate	visual metaphor, an allusion or parody, when historical stories are portrayed in prints in a contemporary manner
mon	crests, including actors' crests, they frequently appear in prints on costumes as an aid to identification
nikuhitsu	original paintings
nishiki-e	'brocade pictures', the full colour print
ōban	print format measuring 39.0 x 27.0 cm
obi	sash, worn around the waist over *kosode*
oiran	high ranking courtesan, prior to the 1750s high ranking courtesans were called *tayū*
shunga	literally 'spring pictures', refers to pictures depicting erotica
sui	to behave in an appropriate manner, the manner of a sophisticate, a prototype of *tsū*
sumizuri-e	monochrome black and white prints
tayū	high ranking courtesans — from the 1750s known as *oiran*
tsū	connoisseurship, a person who was intelligent, amusing and polished and who had a sophisticated knowledge of Yoshiwara etiquette
ukiyo-e	images of 'the floating world', prints and paintings representing urban life during the Edo period
yakusha-e	'actor prints'
yakatabune	'pleasure boats', large-roofed boats which could be hired for private parties and liaisons

SELECT BIBLIOGRAPHY

Addiss, Stephen (ed.), *Japanese Ghosts and Demons: Art of the supernatural*, New York: George Braziller in association with the Spencer Museum of Art, University of Kansas, 1985.

Akiyama, Terukazu, *Treasures of Asia: Japanese painting*, New York: Rizzoli International Publications, 1977.

Casal, U.A., 'Japanese Cosmetics and Teeth Blackening', *Transactions of the Asiatic Society of Japan*, 3rd ser., Supplement to vol. 9, 1966, pp.5–27.

Clark, Timothy, *Ukiyo-e Paintings in the British Museum*, London: British Museum Press, 1992.

Clark, Timothy, *The Art of Kawanabe Kyōsai*, London: British Museum Press, 1993.

Cobb, Jody, *Geisha: The life, the voices, the art*, New York: Alfred A. Knopf, 1995.

Dalby, Liza Crihfield, *Kimono: Fashioning culture*, New York: Yale University Press, 1993.

DeBecker, Joseph Ernest, *The Nightless City or The History of the Yoshiwara Yukwaku*, Rutland: Charles E. Tuttle, 1972.

Deutsch, Sanna Saks, in Howard A.Link, *The Feminine Image: Women of Japan* (exhibition catalogue), Honolulu: Honolulu Academy of Art, 1985.

Gluckman, Dale Carolyn and Takeda, Sharon Sadako (eds), *When Art Became Fashion: Kosode in Edo-period Japan*, Los Angeles and New York: Los Angeles County Museum of Art, Weatherhill, 1992.

Hachmojiya, Jisho, *The Actor's Analects (Yakusha rongo)*, Charles J.Dunn and Bunzō Torigoe (trans.), New York: Columbia University Press, 1969.

Hibbett, Howard, *The Floating World of Japanese Fiction*, London: Oxford University Press, 1959.

Illing, Richard, *Japanese Erotic Art and the Life of the Courtesan*, London: Thames and Hudson, 1978.

Ing, Eric van den and Robert Schaap, *Beauty and Violence: Japanese prints by Yoshitoshi*, Bergeyk: Society for Japanese Arts, 1992.

Jenkins, Donald, *The Floating World Revisited*, Portland: Portland Art Museum in association with University of Hawaii Press, 1993.

Joly, Henri L., *Legend in Japanese Art*, Rutland: Charles E. Tuttle, 7th printing 1983.

Kennedy, Alan, *Japanese Costume History and Tradition*, Paris: Adam Biro, 1990.

Lane, Richard, *Images from the Floating World: The Japanese print*, New York: G.P. Putnam's Sons, 1978.

Lawson, Dawn (ed.), *Undercurrents in the Floating World: Censorship and Japanese prints*, New York: The Asia Society Galleries, 1991.

Seigle, Cecilia Segawa, *Yoshiwara: The glittering world of the Japanese courtesan*, Honolulu: University of Hawaii Press, 1993.

Smith, Lawrence (ed.), *Ukiyoe: Images of unknown Japan*, London: British Museum Publications, 1988.

Stevenson, John, *Yoshitoshi's One Hundred Aspects of the Moon*, Seattle: San Francisco Graphic Society, 1992.

Stevenson, John, *Yoshitoshi's Women: The woodblock print series 'Fuzoku Sanjuniso'*, Boulder: Avery Press, 1986.

Stinchecum, Amanda Mayer, *Kosode: 16th –19th century textiles from the Nomura Collection*, New York: Japan Society and Kodansha International, 1984.

Swinton, Elizabeth de Sabato (ed.), *The Women of the Pleasure Quarter: Japanese paintings and prints of the floating world*, New York: Hudson Hills Press in association with the Worcester Art Museum, Massachusetts, 1996.

Williams, Marjorie, *Japanese Prints: Realities of the 'Floating World'*, Cleveland: The Cleveland Museum of Art in cooperation with Indiana University Press, 1983.